THE TREE OF SPIRIT

THE TREE OF SPIRIT

Essays and Lessons on Tarot, Cabala, and the Spiritual Path

John Gilbert
edited by John Michael Greer

AEON

First published in 2023 by
Aeon Books

Copyright © 2023 by John Gilbert

British Library Cataloguing in Publication Data

A C.I.P. for this book is available from the British Library

ISBN-13: 978-1-80152-072-0

Typeset by vPrompt eServices Pvt Ltd, India

www.aeonbooks.co.uk

CONTENTS

INTRODUCTION

John Gilbert, the author of these essays, was one of many students and teachers of alternative spirituality active in late twentieth and early twenty-first century America. Unlike most of the others, the teachings he had to offer his students did not come from the pop occultism of the post-1960s era. They had older and stranger roots, and it may help readers of this book understand what follows to trace those roots back to their sources.

John was born in 1938 in Pierre, South Dakota and raised in an ordinary Christian household, but his personal spiritual vision called him in other directions from an early age. After a stint in the Coast Guard and four years in college getting a teaching degree, he settled in Colorado with his wife Judith and went to work as a high school teacher. It was there that he met his own spiritual teacher, Rev. Matthew Shaw

Shaw was a Universalist minister in Pennsylvania, part of a denomination that was once a major presence in American religious life but was fading fast in his time. The Universalists, as their name suggests, believe that salvation is universal, because a loving God would not condemn any of His children to eternal torment. This faith in Divine mercy and generosity encouraged Universalists to take up an open-minded attitude toward other religious and spiritual teachings, and Shaw embraced that aspect of the tradition with enthusiasm.

I have not been able to trace the exact nature of Shaw's early studies, but it's clear from the teachings he passed on to John Gilbert that he was familiar with a wide range of American occult traditions. In 1948, after several years of intensive study and devotional practice, he founded an organization called the Modern Order of Essenes. It was one of several organizations of the time that drew inspiration from the Essenes of the time of Jesus, and it taught meditation, prayer, blessing, and spiritual healing to its members. It might have become a significant force in the Universalist Church, but changes were on the horizon.

In 1951, the leadership of the Universalist Church in America voted to begin exploring a merger with the larger and wealthier Unitarian Church. Shaw was one of many Universalist ministers who objected to this project, arguing that the distinctive traditions of the Universalist Church would be erased by the more numerous Unitarian faction. They turned out to be correct—the Unitarian Universalist Association, the church founded by the merger of the two denominations in 1961, preserved nothing of historic Universalism but the name. Long before that happened, however, Shaw and some of his fellow dissidents went their own way.

In 1952 in Allentown, Pennsylvania, Shaw and a fellow Universalist minister, Rev. Omar Zasluchy, were consecrated as bishops in the historic Christian apostolic succession by Bishop Robert Monroe of the Liberal Catholic Church, an independent sacramental church loosely associated with the Theosophical movement. They then consecrated a third Universalist minister, Rev. Owen Symanski, and the three of them founded their own church, the Universal Gnostic Church (UGC). Bishops Zasluchy and Symanski remained in Pennsylvania, but after a few years, Shaw relocated to Colorado to found a UGC church there.

He soon made the acquaintance of an influential figure in the alternative spiritual scene, Dr. Juliet Ashley, a longtime student of Edgar Cayce and Manly P. Hall, who had also studied psychology with Carl Jung in Zurich. Ashley was by then the head of three small esoteric organizations, the Ancient Order of Druids in America, the Order of Spiritual Alchemy, and an American offshoot of the famous Hermetic Order of the Golden Dawn. The two of them became close friends and, as usually happens in the alternative spirituality community, exchanged teachings and initiations: Ashley was consecrated as a bishop in the UGC and passed through the necessary studies and ceremonies to become a Master Essene Healer, while Shaw worked his way through the curricula and initiations of Ashley's three orders, taking on a magical name: Rhodonn Starrus, derived from the Greek for "Rose Cross."

This was the complex body of tradition that John Gilbert received when he began his studies with Rev. Shaw. John added to those teachings from his own studies and experiences, and passed on the result to his students. In the process, he wrote down a good part of what he knew. Some of that material remains the property of the orders for which it was written, and some has apparently been lost, but a great many of his instructional papers have survived. This volume contains some of these.

The first two chapters consist of courses on the spiritual dimensions of the tarot which he wrote for the Tarot Institute, an organization he founded to teach tarot divination to subscribers online. Each of these courses was originally issued one section at a time in the Institute's newsletter, and was intended to provide students with material for meditation and reflection for a week. Students of the material in the companion volume, *The Doors of Tarot*, may find it helpful to read and study these after working with the essays in that book.

The third and fourth chapters are extended essays he wrote on the Cabalistic Tree of Life, a diagram of the deep structure of the cosmos used by many Western esoteric spiritual traditions. The first was originally made available to students of the Magickal Order of the Golden Dawn, John's reworking of the Golden Dawn material he received from Juliet Ashley, while the other explores the Tree of Life from the point of view of spiritual alchemy and was hosted for some years on the Order of Spiritual Alchemy website. The final chapter is a series of essays he wrote exploring the common ground between the Tarot, the Cabalistic Tree of Life, and the traditions of modern Paganism. These three chapters are not divided into bite-sized portions like the first two, but students of Western esoteric spirituality will find plenty worth contemplating in them.

By the time John passed in 2021, the traditions he had inherited were all but forgotten except by small circles of students. It has been an honor as well as a delight to edit them for publication and pass on his teachings to future generations.

—John Michael Greer

CHAPTER 1

The Spiritual Journey

0

Some mystics believe we made a conscious decision to leave the spiritual world where we normally reside to enter the world of matter. We do this to learn more about ourselves and others. So each time we enter the world of matter we have a reason for incarnating, a purpose to fulfill.

According to these mystics, we are not the victims of some ridiculous set of circumstances. We choose to be who we are. We choose to be with the people who bring us into this life and they choose to be a part of our lives. We choose to be born.

We enter into an act of creation and spend the rest of our lives creating who and what we are. We choose the time and place where we will be by the choices we make in our lives. We choose who we become by the choices we make in our lives. We choose how we will react to the circumstances we chose to challenge in our lives. This is how we grow spiritually and this is the Journey of a Lifetime, the Journey of the Fool.

Before we begin our journey we set up the circumstances of our life, we select the challenges we will face, we agree with others to be our parents and our children, our friends and our lovers, and thus we prepare to incarnate in the physical world of matter.

This preparation is represented by the Fool. We dress in a physical body and carry our baggage with us. Our personality comes along as our faithful companion. We step off into the unknown and forget who we are. We've made a willful decision to experience physical reality in this physical universe.

And so we shall. But that's another story represented by the rest of the Major Arcana. We'll continue with the Magician in Part One.

1

The Fool is incarnate in a physical body. For a moment, consider that the Fool is leaving behind perfection and complete freedom to painfully and traumatically enter this world of corruption. The Buddha called this the world of pain and suffering. It is also called the World of Sin.

Whatever it is, the Fool does not know it. The Fool is in a body he or she cannot yet control, looking out at a world he or she does not yet understand. The Fool draws power from above and brings it to this reality. And the Fool pays attention.

The Fool pays attention to everything. This is the first act of creation, paying attention to yourself and the things around you. The Fool is starting to create who he or she will be. The Fool is paying attention.

This first act of self-creation is represented by the Magician who draws energy from above and sends it into this incarnation. The Magician pays attention to everything inside and outside him- or herself. Paying attention is the first key to success in this life.

That's one way of looking at the Magician.

2

The Fool becomes the Magician by paying attention and observing the people and the world around him or her. As the Fool pays attention, the Fool learns, the Fool remembers.

The Fool remembers the people, the faces, the voices, the sounds, and the things that come into the Fool's life. The Fool remembers the smells and the odors, the tastes and the textures of things and people. And in remembering, the Fool knows when the same person or object touches into his or her life.

This second act of self-creation is represented by the High Priestess. It is a subconscious process indicated by the Moons at her feet and on or near her head. The High Priestess remembers everything subconsciously, but only part of that knowledge is remembered consciously as shown by the partially exposed scroll in her hand. Subconscious memory and remembering is the second key to success in life.

That's one way of looking at the High Priestess.

3

The Fool becomes the Magician by paying attention and observing the people and the world around him or her. As the Fool pays attention, the Fool learns, the Fool remembers. The Fool becomes the High Priestess.

Then the Fool does a remarkable thing. The Fool not only observes and remembers the people, the faces, the voices, the sounds, the smells, the tastes and the things that come into the Fool's life. The Fool imagines how all of these things can change. The Fool imagines how things might be better. How they might be different in the future. The Fool imagines how the future might change the people and things in the Fool's life.

This third act of self-creation is represented by the Empress. This is a fruitful process indicated by the condition of the plants around her and the Empress herself. The Empress is fruitful and everything around her is fruitful and it all represents a fruitful imagination. Imagination that can take us on flights of fantasy is that same imagination which creates our own future moment by moment. What we imagine, we can become. What we imagine, we can do. What we imagine is one expression of who we are. Imagination is the third key to success in life.

That's one way of looking at the Empress.

4

The Fool becomes the Magician by paying attention and observing the people and the world around him or her. The Fool becomes the High Priestess by learning and remembering. The Fool becomes the Empress by imagining how the people and things in the Fool's life might change for the better or worse.

Then the Fool begins logically and methodically to reason out his or her circumstances. By paying attention to the details of this life, remembering the results of previous actions, and imagining the possible outcomes, the Fool begins logically and methodically to make decisions based on reason.

Reason is the fourth accomplishment of self-creation. It is based on logic, deduction, and inference. The young child begins to learn "if this, then that." The Fool learns to reason out all the problems posed by life in this physical incarnation. This fourth act of self-creation is represented by the Emperor and is called reason or logical thinking. Reason is the fourth key to success in life.

Reasoning is barren while imagination is fruitful. Logical thinking led us to know the world was round before we could prove that was so. Logic is depicted in the implements surrounding and the demeanor of the Emperor.

That's one way of looking at the Emperor.

5

The Fool learns how to use his or her conscious mind (Magician), subconscious mind (High Priestess), imagination (Empress), and logical and reasoning power (Emperor). Another phenomenon is at work in the Fool's life and though this power can be imagined and remembered, and logically reasoned out by paying attention, it is difficult to pin down and fully explain.

This power uses the same tools of attention, memory and logic but instead of imagination another power is used. This power is not exciting and energetic, it is soft and quiet, calm and peaceful. It takes the Fool into deeper and deeper levels of the events and people in the Fool's life rather than away from the mundane cares of the world on a fantasy trip.

Discovering this inner calm and peaceful power called intuition is the fifth accomplishment of self-creation. It is not something one does like paying attention. Nor is it logical and easy to reason out. It is not something one remembers. Nor is it an exciting and energizing flight of fantasy. It is a small quiet voice the Fool finds within. This fifth act of self-creation is represented by the Hierophant and is called intuition.

Imagination is fruitful and multiplies. Intuition is a seed hidden within all things. Imagination is exciting and takes us away from whatever or whomever is on our minds. Intuition is calm and peaceful and it takes us to deeper and deeper levels of understanding of the things and people in our lives. Imagination shouts to get our attention. Intuition speaks in a small, quiet voice.

This is one way of looking at the Hierophant.

6

The Fool (Superconsciousness) decided to incarnate in this physical reality. The Magician pays attention to him or herself and the things around him or herself. This is self-consciousness. The High Priestess recalls past events. This is subconsciousness. The Empress is the imaginative mind, the Emperor the reasoning mind, and the Hierophant the intuitive mind.

We come now to the Lovers who represent the discriminative mind. This mind differentiates or tells the difference between things ... this is this and that's that. Another name for the Discriminative Mind is Conscience. We know the difference between right and wrong. There's no debate about this. The debate is over whether we'll do what's right or not.

As the Fool develops his or her discriminative mind, he or she is more at peace with the world and the events of this world. When people get into their own reasoning mind, they become "I centered" and very concerned about themselves and how things affect them. If they get into their imaginations, they become excited. Imagination tends to make us excited about the future possibilities. If they get into their subconscious mind they become excited or saddened by past memories.

When you tune into your intuitive mind (Hierophant) you become very calm and peaceful. You just know that what you're receiving is the truth. You don't become emotionally involved with it though you can feel any emotions attached to the insights you receive. That's when your discriminative mind (The Lovers) confirms you are experiencing truth.

That's one way of looking at the Lovers.

7

The Fool has learned how to pay attention to the details in the Fool's life, to become aware of things within and outside. The Fool remembers past details (High Priestess) of life's experiences. The Fool imagines possible futures (Empress) based on self-conscious awareness and past experience. The Fool reasons out possible consequences of imagined futures and present circumstances. The Fool learns to control self-conscious thoughts (Emperor) and wild imaginings. The Fool learns to tell the difference between (The Lovers) the masculine and the feminine, the past and the future, the good and the evil, the right and the wrong.

That brings us to the Seventh Secret of Life, the seventh act of self-creation, the ability to receive Divine influence in our lives. We are forever and always a child of the Divine and the Divine resides within each of us. We are each an individualized expression of the Divine and as such we are in constant communication with the Divine. The problem is we don't always listen, we're not always receptive.

Many Masters in many times have said things similar to what the Master Jesus is quoted as saying in the Gospel of Thomas: "Let him who has ears, hear." We all have inner ears. All we have to do is listen. As we listen to the outer sounds with our outer ears we become aware of ourselves and our surroundings. As we listen to the inner sounds with our inner ears we become aware of who and what we really are and the spiritual world in which we truly reside.

By becoming receptive to Divine influence in our lives we are able to progress along our chosen spiritual path.

That's one way of looking at the Chariot (Key 7).

8

The Fool pays attention (Magician) to his or her subconsciousness (High Priestess) and learns some valuable lessons:

- Subconsciousness always remembers whatever you do, think, or say
- The more emotional the memory the easier it is to remember
- Subconsciousness is not logical, it does not reason, it merely remembers
- Subconsciousness is not imaginative and not self-conscious, it remembers
- Subconsciousness is not intuitive and doesn't discriminate, it remembers
- Subconsciousness is not intuitive and it is not always receptive, it remembers
- Subconsciousness is obedient to our instructions

We instruct our subconsciousness daily by our thoughts, words, and actions. Subconsciousness remembers and helps us continue to think, speak, and act in the same manner. Thus our personal habits are formed. What we have thought, said, and done before is what we will continue to think, speak, and do until and unless we change our subconscious minds.

Key 8, Strength, represents one of the most powerful methods of changing our subconscious thinking patterns. This method is Suggestion. By suggesting that we change our thoughts, words or actions, we will. By suggesting the same things over and over we change more quickly. By suggesting these same changes and emotionally charging our suggestions, we change even more quickly.

Suggestion can take many forms. Affirmations are suggestions we repeat over and over like a mantra with the intention of changing some part or portion of our life. Rituals and meditations can be used to focus on a change we want to make in our life. The things we say, think, and do are all suggestions about how we want our life to be.

Suggestions are personal. They have to do with us as individuals, with changes we want to make in ourselves. We cannot change another human being, we can only change ourselves. To think otherwise is fantasy. To attempt to change ourselves is our duty as we travel the spiritual path.

We can become more than we are today by using the Law of Suggestion in our own life. The Law of Suggestion says that whatever we want to be, whatever we want to do, and whatever we want to express, we can achieve by suggesting the requisite changes to our own subconscious minds. We decide what the suggestion will be. Here are some examples of how you might use affirmations in your life:

- The Eight of Cups means ... (whatever you want it to mean)
- The reversed Seven of Swords means ... (you choose)
- I am paying more and more attention to the people in my life
- My memory of past events is improving day by day
- My imagination is directed by my will more and more each day
- Day by day in every way my breathing is slower, deeper, and calmer
- My intuitive mind becomes active whenever I ask it to do so
- My discriminative powers increase day by day
- My immune system is getting stronger and healthier day by day

Suggestion is the eighth act of self-creation and it is represented by Key 8 "Strength" which usually depicts somebody (you) holding and controlling an animal (animal instincts = subconsciousness) through some hidden power within yourself. That hidden power is Suggestion and it is your strongest weapon for change in your own life. Nothing in this world is as strong as the Power of Suggestion within yourself. It can change who you are, what you do, and how you think. Nothing is as powerful as this.

Suggestion is the eighth level of consciousness and the eighth secret to success in this life. That's one way of looking at Key 8.

9

The Fool (Superconsciousness) has discovered the power of suggestion using Key 8 (Strength). He or she has learned how to change his or her life by using the Law of Suggestion to change old habits and form new ones:

- The Fool's attention to the details of life improves (Magician)
- The Fool's memory is more detailed and precise (High Priestess)
- The Fool's imagination is under control (Empress)
- The Fool's reasoning powers are better (Emperor)
- The Fool's intuition blossoms and flourishes (Hierophant)
- The Fool's power of discrimination is enhanced (Lovers)
- The Fool's ability to receive Divine influence grows (Chariot)
- The Fool applies the Law of Suggestion to all facets of life (Strength)

As a result of this spiritual growth, we are able to identify the World of Opposites that resides within us all on every level of our being. We start to see the good and the bad, the positive and the negative, our strengths and weaknesses, the male and female being within each and every one of us.

More than this, we begin to bring these opposites within ourselves together. We start to balance ourselves, to overcome our weaknesses, to mellow out. We combine our pride and arrogance with humility to take the edge off our harshness. We let our feminine side soften our masculine. We encourage the opposites within ourselves to unite.

This process of Uniting the Opposites within ourselves and becoming a more spiritual person is the ninth act of self-creation depicted by Key 9

(The Hermit). The Hermit is a gentle person filled with unconditional love. He/she is a Light in the World, a Spiritual Beacon for others to follow. The Fool becomes the Hermit. This is our destiny.

We become The Hermit when we embark on the Spiritual Journey and unite the opposites within ourselves. This Union of Opposites is the ninth secret to success in this life.

That's one way of looking at The Hermit.

10

The Fool (Superconsciousness) has discovered how to identify and unite the opposites within (The Hermit). This is sometimes referred to as Enlightenment though it has other names. By whatever name you call it, this is a major step forward on one's spiritual path.

Once a person reaches this point in their spiritual journey they begin to see the world differently. They begin to understand the rules that govern our existence. One of these rules is the Law of Karma,which simply stated says:

- What you do to others you do to yourself
- What goes around comes around
- For every action, there is an equal and opposite reaction
- For every cause, there's an effect
- We receive what we deserve and we deserve what we receive

It's the idea that the thoughts in our heads have power and so do the desires of our hearts. This power causes things to happen the way we think and desire. We receive according to our heart's desire and our mind's imagination. What we think about is what we become. What we desire is what we become. We are in charge of our life on many, many levels.

This concept of receiving what we give is the tenth act of self-creation depicted by Key 10 (The Wheel). The Wheel goes round and round and it represents all the decisions and desires of our life. It represents the results of what we think and desire. We control our own destiny, whether we believe it or not, by what we think, what we do, what we desire, what we imagine, and what we are. This concept is the tenth secret to success in life.

That's one way of looking at The Wheel of Life.

11

The Fool (Superconsciousness) has learned that what goes around comes around by studying the Wheel of Life. Now the Fool makes a really startling discovery, one that's mystified adepts of every religion from time immemorial, one of the hardest lessons in life we'll ever learn, one of the most difficult lessons to really understand with every level of our being. That lesson is that the Universe is perfectly just in all things. What we deserve is what we get, and what we get is exactly what we deserve.

This concept of Universal Justice is almost impossible to understand if we look at the physical world in which we live. People get hurt and they don't deserve to get hurt. People die before their time. Some people are thin and pretty and very nasty. Other people are average-looking and wonderful, truly wonderful people. But that's only the beginning.

Women work harder and get paid less than men. Blacks go to jail much more often for the same crime than whites. People accept the persecution of Jews and Orientals more easily than the persecution of Christians. Discrimination and not Justice rules the lives of Pagans, Gays, and the poor. So how can there be Universal Justice?

Resolving these questions and problems is the work of Key 11. Looking beyond this physical reality to the underlying reality which is often called the Foundation of the World and using our intuition, imagination, reasoning powers, and discrimination is how we'll start to understand the truth of the undeviating justice of the universe.

We can't get bogged down in the unfairness of life. We have to look beyond that, look deeper. All people have free will and some choose to hurt others and you'll never find any justice in that. Things over which we have no control do happen. They just happen and people get hurt and you'll never find any justice in that. Look deeper.

Here's a big hint we learn from the study of Gnosticism and Alchemy: When you look behind this thing we call reality, you discover it's all an illusion. You and I and everything are living spirits unaffected by the events of this world. Each of us is an eternal, individualized expression of the Divine. Right now we live in the World of Illusion for our own edification. It's not what happens to us in the world that counts but how we react to what happens to us. It's not who we are right now but who are becoming that really matters.

This process of looking for perfect Justice in the Universe is the eleventh act of self-creation depicted by Key 11 (Justice). When we discover the true meaning of Justice we experience the eleventh secret to achieving success in this life. That's one way of looking at Justice (whether Key 8 or Key 11 is Justice).

12

The Fool (Superconsciousness) has learned the Universe is unfailingly just in all things (Justice). Once the Fool really understands all the various ramifications of this knowledge, the Fool experiences a reversal in his or her thinking. This reversal (Hanged Man) is so complete that the Fool cannot act in an evil way toward anything or anybody. The Fool is unswerving in serving good in all things and unconditionally loves everything.

The Fool no longer fears death nor living. All fear has been destroyed. The Fool no longer becomes angry at people, things, or events. All anger has been destroyed. The Fool is content with life as it is and strives always to make it better for one and all. The Fool no longer sees the separation of spirituality and physicality but sees the spirituality in all there is, all that ever has been, and all that will ever be—even you and me.

The process of reversing one's thinking about life and the important things in one's life is the twelfth act of self-creation depicted by Key 12 (the Hanged Man). When we discover the true meaning of life we reverse our thinking and this is the twelfth secret to achieving success in this life.

That's one way of looking at the Hanged Man (Key 12).

13

The Fool (Superconsciousness) has reversed his or her thinking about life and self (Hanged Man) and now sees the bigger picture. The Fool understands that we're all in this life together and how we interact with each other really matters. This transformation (Death) is complete. The old us dies to this world and a new us is born. We are no longer who and what we once were. We are changed. We completely change our behavior toward all people, places, and things. We are reborn. We rise above the dross.

The Fool is no longer selfish but becomes generous in all things. The Fool overcomes the seven vices of pride, anger, lust, greed, jealousy, gluttony, and laziness. The Fool becomes other-centered, unconditionally loving, peaceful, virtuous, trusting, and temperate. As with all things spiritual, this change may be gradual or it may come as in a flash of lightning. However long it takes, we become a changed person and we change our behavior toward everything.

This process of transforming who and what we are is the thirteenth act of self-creation depicted by Key 13 (Death). When we become changed persons we achieve our true potential and this is the thirteenth secret to achieving success in this life.

That's one way of looking at Death (Key 13).

14

The Fool (Superconsciousness) has transformed him- or herself (Death) and is now a different person than before. Some people never change. They leave this world much the same as they entered it. It takes a very strong person to travel the Path of the Fool, to take a spiritual journey. It takes a lot of hard work and determination to become the Fool.

As we journey through the first seven cards we begin to understand who and what we are. But this is only the beginning. As we travel through the next seven cards we learn how to suggest (Key 8) how we can change our life. We unite the opposites within ourselves (Key 9). We begin to understand how the things we do, think, and say change who and what we are (Key 10). We learn about the undeviating justice of the Universe (Key 11). We reverse our way of thinking about all things (Key 12). We change who and what we are (Key 13).

Then we stop and verify that all of this is true (Key 14). We look inside ourselves to see if we've really changed, if we've changed our minds about things, if our behavior really is different, if we really are new and different persons, if we're really more spiritual. We verify truth and know we're not fooling ourselves. We verify each step we've taken and know exactly what we've done. We learn the truth about ourselves. This process of verifying who and what we have become is the fourteenth act of self-creation depicted by Key 14 (Temperance). We verify for ourselves and all humankind that we've become a changed person and we begin to think, act, and speak as this new person and this is the fourteenth secret to achieving success in this life.

That's one way of looking at Temperance (Key 14).

15

The Fool has now completed the first two-thirds of his or her journey and now embarks on the final leg (the last one-third). If you don't understand where the Fool has traveled, you might want to review the material for at least Keys 14 and 7.

To understand the rest of the journey you may want to place the following three cards in a vertical column with the numbers running from top to bottom. We're going to start with these three cards:

- 1—Magician
- 7—Strength
- 15—Devil

The Magician observes the outer world (Key 1) and eventually learns to use the art of suggestion (Key 8) to change him- or herself. The things the Fool suggests to him- or herself eventually come to pass and the Fool is tied to the results of this suggestion (Key 15).

This bondage can tie the Fool down if the suggestion used by the Fool was for things in this physical world. You receive what you ask for and with these things come responsibilities unique to those things.

Whatever it is you desire strongly, by using the power of Key 8 you get it, and with it comes the responsibility for it. This is bondage. This is being chained to the house, chained to the car, chained to the job, chained to the family, chained to whatever it is you suggested to yourself, you wanted. This is the Devil at its grossest level.

If you want spiritual enlightenment and you use this same power (Keys 1 and 8) you will attain spiritual enlightenment and all the freedom that comes with it. Notice that now it's freedom rather than bondage. Notice something about the bondage indicated in Key 15 for the deck or decks of your choice. In almost every instance the bonds are loose. They can be removed. We can exercise our own free will and change.

This realization of our own voluntary bondage to the things of our choice based on our previous observations and self-suggestions is the fifteenth act of self-creation depicted by Key 15 (the Devil). The knowledge that we can change this ourselves by reversing the process is the fifteenth secret to achieving success in this life.

That's one way of looking at The Devil (Key 15).

16

The Fool pays attention to his or her own body and the things going on around him- or herself. He or she uses this information to suggest changes in his or her life. This process of change results in the Fool being tied down to his or her desires. The end result is Bondage. Responsibility for the things the Fool wanted ties the Fool down to those things (Keys 1, 8, 15)

So the Fool tries a different tactic by relying on his or her memory track or subconscious memory (Key 2) and uniting the opposites within him- or herself (Key 9). The Fool remembers everything he or she has tried in the past and recalls the results of each attempt. Then the Fool combines the positive and the negative, the good and the bad, the opposites within. The result is a dramatic change in who and what the Fool is based on a deep and thorough self-evaluation.

To understand this part of the journey you may want to place the three cards being discussed in a vertical column with the numbers running from top to bottom. We're using these three cards:

- 2—High Priestess
- 9—The Hermit
- 16—The Tower

This dramatic change is sometimes called the "Dark Night of the Soul," or merely "Mid-life Crisis." By whatever name, it's a very rough time indeed. It's a time of internal turmoil as the individual goes through his or her memories of the past, examining the successes and the failures, the good and the bad.

It doesn't need to be so traumatic, so singularly devastating. It can be a methodical step-by-step self-analysis in an atmosphere of unconditional love, of total and unreserved self-acceptance. Thus we find the "Golden Mean Within" or the "Middle Way." We balance ourselves, the positive and negative, the masculine and feminine, the good and bad.

This process of remembering all we have been and all we've done and then balancing all of these things, uniting these opposites within ourselves, is the sixteenth act of self-creation depicted by Key 16 (The Tower) and this is the sixteenth secret to achieving success in this life.

That's one way of looking at the Tower (Key 16).

17

For the rest of this journey you may find it helpful to lay out the Major Arcana in what is normally referred to as the "Golden Dawn Tableau." This is accomplished by laying out the cards in three rows in numbered sequence from left to right with the Fool placed above Key 4 in the first row. It looks like this:

- Row one is Keys 1 through 7
- Row two is Keys 8 through 14
- Row three is Keys 15 through 21

The Fool is in a row all by itself above Key 4 and above Row One.

We've already examined the first two vertical rows on the left on our discussions of Keys 15 and 16 (the Devil and the Tower). Now we examine the third vertical row from the left and at the same time we'll consider the first three vertical rows together as a block.

The first three cards in the top row are the Magician (Key 1), the High Priestess (Key 2), and the Empress (Key 3). The message of these three cards is that by paying attention (Key 1) to our subconscious mind (Key 2) we develop our imagination (Key 3). The better we pay attention the better we develop our imagination, and the more we're able to control it and direct it. The less attention we pay to our subconscious mind the more uncontrollable our imagination becomes.

The first three cards in the middle row are Strength (Key 8), the Hermit (Key 9), and the Wheel (Key 10). The message of these cards is that by suggesting (Key 8) how to combine the opposites within ourselves (Key 9) we're able to control our own destiny (Key 10). The first three cards in the final row are Devil (Key 15), Tower (Key 16), and Star (Key 17). The message of these cards is that when our desire to relieve ourselves of bondage (Key 15) to this physical world becomes so great we change ourselves in an instant (Key 16), the truth of all things is revealed (Key 17) to us, and we are free from the constraints we formerly placed upon ourselves.

That's the message of the Left Pillar, which the ancients called Boaz or the pillar of Strength, and which is depicted in Tarot, the Tree of Life, and Masonry as a black pillar. Thus these nine cards deliver the message of the Black Pillar, the message of our dark side. For if these things are perverted, evil will manifest itself in our lives.

Looking now at the third vertical row, we have the Empress above the Wheel and the Star beneath:

- 3—The Empress
- 10—The Wheel
- 17—The Star

The message of these three cards is that our imagination, when properly used to control our karma, reveals truth in all things to us. We now have two paths leading to personal revelation. But there's a third. We can travel that "path less traveled" by paying attention (Key 1) to the opposites combining within ourselves (Key 9) and the truth will be revealed as well. This diagonal path leads to the same truth as the other two. To the true mystic, both the diagonal (Magician–Hermit–Star) and the horizontal (Devil–Tower–Star) paths are there to help the traveler travel imaginatively (Empress) through his or her personal karma (Wheel) to the truth of all things (Star).

This process of imagining all we can be as we resolve all our karmic debts, which reveals the truth of all things to us, is the seventeenth act of self-creation depicted by Key 17 (The Star) and this is the seventeenth secret to achieving success in this life.

That's one way of looking at The Star (Key 17).

18

The second group of three cards in the top row are the High Priestess (Key 2), the Empress (Key 3), and the Emperor (Key 4). The message of these three cards is that our subconscious mind (Key 2) acting through our imagination (Key 3) gives birth to our reasoning power (Key 4).

The second group of three cards in the middle row are the Hermit (Key 9), the Wheel (Key 10), and the Justice (Key 11). The message of these cards is that by combining the opposites within ourselves (Key 9) and by controlling our own destiny (Key 10) we are able to attain complete balance or equilibration (Key 11) in our lives.

The second group of three cards in the bottom row are the Tower (Key 16), The Star (Key 17), and The Moon (Key 18). The message of these cards is that when we change ourselves in an instant (Key 16) and the truth of all things is revealed (Key 17) to us, we organize (Key 18) our lives for the spiritual awakening we are about to attain.

The fourth column in our twenty-one card tableau of the Major Arcana contains the cards:

- The Emperor (Key 4)
- Justice (Key 9)
- The Moon (Key 18)

This means that when we apply our reasoning skills (Key 4) to becoming completely balanced within ourselves (Key 11) we become completely organized (Key 18). Becoming completely balanced within ourselves is the "Mystical Marriage" of our masculine and feminine sides. The feminine side we already know is the Black Pillar. Soon we'll learn the masculine side is the White Pillar. When these become balanced within us we are said to travel the Middle Road, the Middle Way, that Path Less Traveled.

The Ancients attributed the process of sleep to this mystical marriage and sleep was considered to be the "Small Death" because we came back from it each morning. In this process of the Small Death they saw a preview of the Big Death from which we come back each lifetime.

The mystical question that arises from all this is "Are we really alive now? or is this the death from which we will be reborn into the true reality of life?" The Moon posits this question. It asks if this is really a reality or if this is the dream from which we will someday awaken.

The fourth column also includes the Fool above and this is us as we move down the Middle Pillar into manifestation and up the Middle Pillar to our Point of Beginning while moving neither to our right onto the White Pillar nor to the left onto the Black Pillar. That's the message of the Middle Pillar which the ancients called Yod Heh Vau Heh or Jehovah, the secret name of Deity whose true pronunciation and meaning are unknown to us. The root of this Pillar, the foundation of this Pillar if you will, is organizing ourselves for the final steps in our Spiritual Journey toward perfection. This process of organizing ourselves for the final steps of our Spiritual Journey is the eighteenth act of self-creation depicted by Key 18 (the Moon) and this is the eighteenth secret to achieving success in this life.

That's one way of looking at The Moon (Key 18).

19

As we look at the Tableau of twenty-one Major Arcana (plus the Fool above for a total of twenty-two cards) arranged in three rows of seven cards each, we note the third column from the right is the Hierophant (Key 5) with the Hanged Man (Key 12) below and the Sun (Key 19) at the bottom of that column. This means Intuition (Key 5) changes our way of thinking about ourselves (Key 12) and we become Enlightened (Key 19). Being Enlightened means we understand everything. We know why we were born and we know our life's purpose.

Light is an esoteric word meaning knowledge. To gain Light is to gain knowledge. To become Enlightened is to be knowledgeable, to know the truth.

The two cards before the Hierophant are the Emperor and the Empress, Reason and Imagination. That means we have to use our reasoning ability and our imagination in order to develop our intuitive faculties.

The two cards before the Hanged Man are the Wheel and Justice. We attain a change in thinking only after we realize that everything in the world is as it should be and in the final analysis the world is fair.

The two cards preceding the Sun are the Star and the Moon. We need to have hope and faith to tread through the World of Illusion in order to attain Enlightenment.

To attain Enlightenment (Key 19) we need to open our Third Eye and use our Intuitive Mind (Key 5) to help us Change our Thinking (Key 12) about who and what we really are. When we do this, we understand to the very depths of our Soul that we are Divine beings temporarily living in this mortal world for a specific purpose which is our life's goal. We learn and understand that goal.

The Sun (Key 19) teaches us to use our reasoning ability (Key 4) and imagination (Key 3) to empower our intuition (Key 5). Then the Sun (Key 19) teaches us to use our intuition to change our thinking (Key 12) about who and what we are.

That's one way of looking at The Sun (Key 19).

20

As we look at the Tableau of twenty-one Major Arcana arranged in three rows of seven cards each, we note the second column from the right is the Lovers (Key 6) with Death (Key 13) below and Judgment (Key 20) at the bottom of that column. This means that discrimination (Key 6) between this and that, right and wrong so greatly transforms (Key 13) our way of thinking and doing that we realize (Key 20) the truth of all things. We understand everything in our physical, emotional, mental, intuitional, and spiritual worlds. We know the truth and the Creator.

The basis of all Gnostic religions is the faith that the individual can know the Creator whom we call Allah, Jehovah, Adonai, Brahman, Green Man, God, and hundreds or even thousands of other names. By whatever name we call him, her, or it, when we reach this point in our spiritual journey we know him, her, or it on a personal and intimate basis. This is what we call realization. It means we realize the truth. We know God.

Let's look at the two cards which come before Judgment. Key 18 tells us to organize ourselves, our bodies, minds, emotions, intuitions, and spirits. Key 19 promises that if we do these things we'll become regenerated, we'll become once again that which we were. Key 20 now tells us that when we become regenerated we attain that state known as Realization. We remember the truth about all things.

Thus in all Western Mystery Schools, the Sun and the Moon light the way and we realize the Truth. Learning the Truth is the twentieth act of self-creation and the twentieth secret to achieving success in this life. It's a conscious decision we made when we reached the Moon and the Sun that leads us to the Truth in all things.

To more fully understand the message of Keys 6 and 13, let's look at the two cards preceding each of them. The Emperor tells us to reason things out and the Hierophant teaches us to use our intuition.

The promise of these two cards is that if we do these things we'll learn how to discriminate (Lovers) between all things.

Justice teaches us to balance all things in our lives and the Hanged Man instructs us to reverse our thinking about life and things. The promise of these two cards is that if we do these things we'll become transformed (Death). It is this new "us," (Death) which discriminates (Lovers) between things at these spiritual heights, which attains realization (Judgment) in this lifetime.

That's one way of looking at Judgment (Key 20).

21

As we look at the Tableau of twenty-one Major Arcana arranged in three rows of seven cards each, the right-hand column is The Chariot (Key 7) with the Temperance (Key 14) below it and The World (Key 21) at the bottom. This means our ability to receive Divine influence (Key 7) in our lives and to verify the truth (Key 14) of this Divine influence results in our attainment of Cosmic Consciousness (Key 21).

In other words, if we use our Intuition (Key 5) and Discrimination (Key 6) we'll receive Divine Influence (Key 7); and if we change our thinking (Key 12) and our behavior (Key13) accordingly, we'll be able to verify (Key 14) that who and what we really are is an eternal spirit living in this physical reality. Once we attain Enlightenment (Key 19) and Realization (Key 20) we can also use the Divine influence to verify that we've achieved Cosmic Consciousness.

The nine cards in three rows and three columns on the right-hand side of this Tableau represent the Right Pillar on the Tree of Life which the ancients called Jachin or the pillar of Mercy, and which is depicted in Tarot, the Tree of Life, and Masonry as a white pillar. Thus these nine cards deliver the message of the White Pillar, the message of our light side. For if we pay attention to these things we'll attain Cosmic Consciousness and become what we really are—a Divine spirit temporarily living in the world of matter.

Cosmic Consciousness is the state in which we began our spiritual journey as the Fool, but with one exception. We came into this physical reality only after passing through the Veil of Forgetfulness. We've now "torn asunder" this Veil and we no longer live in Ignorance. We live as the eternal spirit we always were all along. We've achieved the end of our spiritual quest, we've achieved Cosmic Consciousness (Key 21). We've come back home to the place we left when we entered this physical reality.

That's one way of looking at the World (Key 21).

22

Spiritual journeys are of several different kinds. We discussed the kind of spiritual journey that takes us back to our Source, to the One Creative Influence in the Universe as we discussed the upright keys. Now we discuss a movement away from that one Source, a journey into the gross physical.

More than anything, following this system being suggested here, the inverted, or reversed, Major Arcana card is a warning that we're going in the wrong direction on our spiritual journey. It's a warning that we're becoming deeper and deeper involved in the physical realities of this life and need to take a look at where we think we're going and what we think we're doing spiritually.

The Magician (Key 1) tells us to pay attention to what's happening in our World. The inverted Magician cautions us that we're paying too much attention to ourselves and not enough attention to our spiritual journey. All spiritual journeys are individual in nature but they all require us to give of ourselves, to help others along the way.

The High Priestess (Key 2) represents an open subconscious mind where every event, thought, and feeling of our existence is recorded for us to use when we need it. The inverted High Priestess warns that we're shutting ourselves off from this valuable memory record which could help us if we but used it.

The Empress (Key 3) is our imagination which we use to imagine possible futures based on our present situation and our memory of past events. It is our most valuable tool for planning our future. But the inverted Empress warns we're letting our imagination go wild. We're spending too much time imagining future events and forgetting to reason them out, to pay attention, and to remember.

The Emperor (Key 4) is our conscious mind, where we reason out problems and the events of our life. Our conscious mind operates in the present. It works with our subconscious mind to bring past memories into the present and it works with our imagination to plan the future. It works with the Magician to pay attention and it works with the

Lovers to tell the difference between things. In the inverted position, the Emperor warns that these things are not being done, that there's a problem with the way we're running our life.

The Hierophant (Key 5) is our intuitive mind which hides when we have an active mind and imagination. But it blossoms when we quiet our mind (Emperor) and imagination (Empress) and quietly pay attention (Magician) using our subconscious mind as a channel for our own higher consciousness, Superconsciousness, (The Fool). The inverted Hierophant warns that we're shutting down our intuitive mind and not allowing our subconscious channel to be open to our own Higher Self and the Universe.

The Lovers (Key 6) help us tell the difference between things. This ability to differentiate between things is the highest power of our reasoning mind (The Emperor) just as our ability to attend to the things around us (The Magician) is the lower power of our rational or cognitive mind. The inverted Lovers warns us that we're not paying attention to the differences between things, that we're not looking for the differences.

The Chariot (Key 7) represents our ability to receive power, energy and instruction from the Universe. It's our receptivity and this depends on all the Keys we've discussed so far. The inverted Chariot indicates we've shut ourselves off from the Universe and refuse to receive knowledge, wisdom, love, and understanding from above.

Strength (Key 8) represents one of the most powerful methods of changing our subconscious thinking patterns. This method is Suggestion. By suggesting change to our inner self we can affect changes in our life. The inverted Key 8 indicates we are not successfully suggesting positive changes in our life.

The Hermit (Key 9) is a gentle person filled with unconditional love because he or she has successfully faced and overcome obstacles and united the opposites in his or her personality and life. The inverted Key 9 suggests our unwillingness to overcome our obstacles and become an example for others to follow.

The Wheel (Key 10) teaches us that we receive what we give, and the Universe treats us as we treat others. The inverted Key 10 indicates our unwillingness to accept this Universal Law and perhaps try to receive better than we give.

Justice (Key 11) says everything in this world is fair and just, the world is as it is because that's the way it's supposed to be. The inverted

Key 11 says we see ourselves as victims and want to blame others for our problems.

The Hanged Man (Key 12) represents a change in thinking about who and what we really are and who and what everything else in this world actually is. The inverted Key 12 represents resistance to accepting the truth about ourselves, resistance to changing our thinking.

Death (Key 13) represents a change in our behavior toward ourselves and all other people, places, and things based on our change in our previous attitude toward ourselves, other people, places, and things. The inverted Key 13 is a wake-up call reminding us we need to change our behavior.

The Temperance (Key 14) tells us to verify the truth of everything we learn about ourselves and Divinity. The inverted Key 14 indicates we are accepting things on faith and not verifying the truth of them for us. Each of us has a responsibility to verify possible truths and arrive at the real truth of the matter.

The Devil (Key 15) reminds us that we're tied down to this physical reality by our own decision. We have the ability to break free of our bonds at any time but we choose not to do so. The inverted Key 15 says we don't even remember making this decision and we don't believe we can ever be free of all this physical weight.

The Tower (Key 16) indicates we can awaken from our ignorance any time we choose to do so, and this awakening will be sudden and overturn our world as we know it. The inverted Key 16 indicates that we enjoy living in ignorance and will not willingly change, but change is inevitable anyway.

The Star (Key 17) says the truth will be revealed to us after we awaken and change our lives. And this truth will set us free. The inverted Key 17 says we're not ready to know the truth about ourselves and all other things.

The Moon (Key 18) tells us to organize our lives and prepare for cosmic awareness, to prepare for Divine communion. Inverted Key 18 tells us to organize our lives even though we don't think we can and warns us not to continue living an unorganized life.

The Sun (Key 19) promises us we'll be regenerated into a new spiritual self if we do these things. The inverted Key 19 warns us we'll never attain cosmic consciousness unless we do regenerate ourselves and our lives.

The Judgment (Key 20) prepares us for realization, for the end of our spiritual quest which is to unite with the Creator of All Things and become One with All. Inverted, Key 20 warns us we don't realize the truth about ourselves, about who and what we really are.

The World (Key 21) is the end of our spiritual quest where we attain union with our creator and experience Cosmic Consciousness. Inverted, Key 21 warns us that we're missing out on this wonderful opportunity and suggests we travel a spiritual path to this end.

Thus ends one way of looking at the inverted cards of the Major Arcana. There are many ways to interpret these cards and we hope this journey has helped you to understand the Major Arcana more completely. We recommend that you find a method of handling the Major Arcana that suits you; one you're comfortable with and one that works for you. We do not recommend you copy our approach and adopt it for your own. Rather, we suggest you take what works for you, add your own twists and turns and make it your own. Then use it.

CHAPTER 2

Universal Laws

1

The first Universal Law we'll discuss is the Law of Unconsciousness which controls how we function in this life. Our Unconscious Mind has many facets. The first is our Autonomic Nervous System (ANS) which controls our heart rate, blood pressure, respiration, digestion and elimination, body temperature, perspiration, and all the other automatic functions of our body.

In general we have very little control over our ANS most of the time though we can control our breath somewhat, cool or heat our body to control temperature and perspiration, and control our intake to control our digestion and elimination. A few yogis and others have also learned how to control their pulse and blood pressure for at least a short period of time.

A second facet of our Unconscious Mind is our automatic responses to stimuli such as heat or cold, loud noises, bright lights, pain, and unfamiliar or undesirable tastes or smells. We have almost no control over these reflexes. That's why they're called "automatic."

A third facet of our Unconscious Mind is learned responses which we allow our Unconscious Mind to do automatically for us such as typing, using a number pad, walking, riding or driving. This includes any learned activity, desire, craving, or addiction. That may explain why men drool when a pretty woman walks into the room, or why a woman preens when a gorgeous hunk walks by.

All of our habits, good, bad, or indifferent, are part of this facet of our Unconscious Mind. Here also lurks the Shadow which we either try to deny or avoid.

A fourth facet of our Unconscious Mind is our Corporeal Mind which is how we control our body. The Corporeal Mind is how we can affect such things as reducing pain, balancing our body, relieving pressure on any part of our body through conscious intervention, or even consciously controlling our respiration or heart rate. We use our Corporeal Mind to calm and relax our body in preparation for meditation and exercise. We consciously relax our muscles, relieve discomfort and prepare our body to take care of itself for the period of our meditation or exercise. This is the first step in using and communicating with our Intuitive Mind. It works like this:

1. Find a quiet place and remove or turn off all possible distractions
2. Sit or recline in a comfortable position
3. Consciously examine your body for any discomfort and relieve it
4. Consciously breathe deeply and continue to relax your body
5. Continue for a few moments or minutes

When you reach a very calm and peaceful state you've reached Stage One which is a preparation state for Meditation. This is not meditation but it sure is peaceful, refreshing, and energizing. Universal Law One is represented by Key 1, The Magician, who uses all sorts of magickal means to keep your body functioning whether you know it or not. If we apply the first Universal Law to the first key, we arrive at the following keywords, phrases, or concepts:

- Pay attention to bodily discomforts and tension
- Pay attention to your unconscious activities
- Pay attention to the things happening around you
- Pay attention to your spiritual path
- Pay attention

If you'd like to take this one step farther, assign the Aces to have the same meaning as The Magician except that meaning applies to the Ace's suit and your keywords, phrases, or concepts for that suit. If Wands are "career" then the Ace of Wands would indicate you need to "pay attention to your career."

The First Universal Law is very important because it forms the basis for meditation, divination, and especially reading tarot cards.

2

Universal Law Two simply states the fact that Subconsciousness, or your subconscious mind, remembers everything infallibly. This means our subconscious mind never makes a mistake. It may be mistaken if we misinform it, but it remembers exactly what we told it. It always remembers exactly what we saw, heard, thought, wrote or said.

If our subconscious mind is a perfect memory bank, we have a very powerful tool for using tarot cards available to us. All we have to do is tell our own subconscious mind what we want each card to mean. We tell our subconscious mind the keywords, phrases, or concepts we want to use for each card and it remembers what we write down or tell it.

A second facet of our subconscious mind is that it controls and overrides our Unconscious Mind. Most of the time our Subconscious Mind lets our Unconscious Mind do its thing and doesn't bother it. But, in an emergency or when it wants to take control, our Subconscious Mind can and does take control of our Unconscious Mind.

This happens during divination. Our Subconscious Mind knows the answer to the question we're trying to answer. It also knows the meanings of the Tarot cards as we've defined those cards. In order to communicate with us using these tarot cards, our Subconscious Mind takes control of our Unconscious Mind and arranges the Tarot cards in just the right order for us to do this reading.

It doesn't matter what method of shuffling the cards we use and it doesn't matter how we select the cards or how we turn them face up on the table. Our Subconscious Mind is in control and brings to each position in the spread we're using just the right card to give us the correct answer. But this happens only if we and our Subconscious Mind are in full agreement as to how the cards will be shuffled, cut, selected, and turned.

Our Subconscious Mind remembers the definitions and instructions we've given it. It never makes a mistake. So, if we follow our own directions, our Subconscious Mind will always give us the correct answer. Problems arise when we do something different than what we've told our Subconscious Mind we were going to do. When we shuffle the cards differently, or cut the cards differently, or select the cards differently, or even turn them differently than what we said we were going to do, we mess up the reading. We get the wrong card in the wrong place at the wrong time and we give our clients the wrong information and bad advice.

No problems arise when we do exactly what we said we were going to do. Our Subconscious Mind gives us the right card in the right position at the right time to give our clients the right answers and good advice. The secret to doing good tarot readings has more to do with how well we communicate with our Subconscious Mind and follow our own directions than it has with the definitions we decide to use with our tarot deck. Subconsciousness always follows our directions and never makes a mistake.

One of the best times to communicate with our Subconscious Mind is when our body is in a very calm and peaceful state like that we reach in Stage One which we discussed in the previous lesson. If we take the time to write down what we wish to communicate to our Subconscious Mind, then enter Stage One and read these things to our Subconscious Mind, our Subconscious Mind will always remember. Now all we have to do is remember what we told our Subconscious Mind.

Here's a secret: When we're in Stage One, our Subconscious Mind will help us remember what we told it. When we're in Stage One it's easier for us to remember what we told our Subconscious Mind.

The secret to using tarot cards for divination is to:

1. Select a tarot deck you like and respect, the one you want to use
2. Take care of this deck according to the rituals you decide to use
3. Shuffle this deck the way you decide to shuffle it
4. Cut the deck the way you want to cut it (if at all)
5. Use the spreads you want to use
6. Select the cards the way you want to select them
7. Turn the cards over the way you want to turn them over

Make these decisions and then inform your Subconscious Mind of these decisions. Your Subconscious Mind will always remember these instructions and will always follow them until you change the rules by changing these instructions. All you have to do is remember the rules yourself. Writing them down in your tarot journal is a good idea.

The secret of being a good tarot reader is to:

1. Define the cards the way you want to define them with the keywords, phrases, or concepts you want to use
2. Tell your Subconscious Mind these definitions
3. Remember what definitions you told your Subconscious Mind
4. Writing them down in your Tarot Journal is a good idea
5. Decide if you're going to use reversals, dignities, or whatever
6. Tell your Subconscious Mind these rules and definitions
7. Remembering what you told your Subconscious Mind is a good idea
8. Writing these down in your Tarot Journal is a good idea
9. Practice doing readings as much as you can

Universal Law Two is represented by Key 2, the High Priestess, who remembers perfectly everything we see, hear, think, write, or speak. If we apply the Second Universal Law to Key 2, we arrive at the following keywords, phrases, or concepts:

• Remember where you are on your spiritual path
• Remember what you say, hear, think, read, and write
• Remember the important things
• Remember

If you'd like to go one step further, assign the pip card two to have the same meaning as the Second Universal Law except the meaning applies to the elements rather than your spiritual path. If Cups are relationships, then the Two of Cups tells you to "remember your relationship."

The Second Universal Law is important because it forms the basis for meditation, divination, and especially reading tarot cards.

3

Universal Law Three simply states the fact the human Imagination, or your Imaginative Mind is unbounded and can imagine anything, and what you imagine becomes reality. This means we can imagine anything we want to imagine. But it also says what we imagine will happen does happen. The reality we live in today is a direct result of what we imagined in the past plus a whole lot of things we don't think we ever imagined.

Psychologists tell us what we fear is what happens. If we're afraid of falling, we fall. If we're afraid of being hurt, we get hurt. If we're afraid of losing something, we lose it. Whatever we fear occupies our imagination. Whatever occupies our imagination, happens. It becomes part of our reality.

Psychology also teaches us what we desire, we obtain. The things in life we most desire, occupy our imagination. Whatever occupies our imagination comes to fruition. It happens. It becomes real.

Imagination is a very powerful tool because it controls our future just as perfectly as our subconsciousness records our past. We cannot do or become what we cannot imagine we can do or become. This is a Universal Law.

In order to become anything, we must first be able to imagine we can become just that. In order to do anything, we must first imagine we can do that. How many people do you know who say they can't do something and they can't do it? How many times have you said you'd do something but you didn't believe you could? Did you do it? How many times have you told yourself you couldn't do it and you couldn't?

Here's a secret. Just about anybody can do anything they put their mind to doing. If you put your mind to learning to read tarot cards, you will learn. If you put your mind to being a professional tarot reader, you will become a professional tarot reader. If you say you can't, you're absolutely right, you can't.

If you put your mind to learning anything, you will learn. If you put your mind to doing anything, you will do it. It's all part of your Imagination!

You can be a tarot reader. You can write tarot books and reviews. You can create your own tarot system. You can create your own tarot deck. You can attain your dreams if you can imagine yourself attaining them. Anything you imagine, you can attain. Anything you can imagine about yourself, you can become.

How? Imagine the possibilities. Put your mind to it. Do what you need to do to achieve your goals. Imagine yourself attaining these goals then go out and achieve them just like you imagined you would.

Go back to the last lesson and review "The Secret to Using Tarot Cards for Divination." Imagine you can do this. Decide how you want to do it and imagine yourself doing it that way. Then just do it. Let your Imagination be your guide.

Then review "The Secret of Being a Good Tarot Reader" and imagine you can do this as well. Imagine the possibilities. Imagine yourself doing what you want to do. Then do it. Follow your Imagination. It will lead you where you want to go.

Are there any pitfalls along the way? Sure. If you imagine yourself failing, you will. If you imagine difficulties, they will appear. If you become convinced you can't do it, you won't. Whatever you can imagine, will happen.

Universal Law Three is represented by Key 3, the Empress, who is the most fruitful thing in the Universe. If we apply the Third Universal Law to Key 3, we arrive at the following keywords, phrases, or concepts:

- Imagine only the things you want to happen to you
- Imagine the possibilities of all you can attain and all you can become
- Imagine how you want your spiritual life to be
- Imagine how you want any part of your life to be
- Imagine the possibilities

If you'd like to go one step further, assign the pip card threes to have the same meaning as the Third Universal Law except the meaning applies to the elements rather than your spiritual path.

The Third Universal Law is important because it forms the basis of what you will become in the future.

4

Universal Law Four indicates we have the innate ability to reason things out for ourselves, to make decisions regarding our life and to base those decisions on our unconscious, subconscious, and imaginative minds. When we use this faculty in this manner we are said to be rational. Hence our thinking mind is often called our rational mind. It's also called our conscious mind.

But if we make decisions without engaging our subconscious and imaginative minds, we're said to be irrational. If we don't apply the lessons we've learned in the past, and if we don't imagine all the consequences of our decisions, we're an irrational person. We act out of instincts or impulses stored in our unconscious mind.

When we reason things out and arrive at the best decision we're capable of making, we can be right or we can be wrong. We can make mistakes. We can err. Even if we make the correct decision we can still be mistaken.

The ability to reason is not infallible. Our subconscious mind may remember everything infallibly but that doesn't mean our conscious mind will act on those memories without error. Psychology teaches us that self-empowered people learn from their mistakes. People who do not learn from their mistakes, who keep making the same mistakes over and over, are mentally challenged. We have the opportunity to learn more by making mistakes than we learn by getting it right. Right is often more fun though.

Our thinking mind, our rational mind, is our conscious mind. As our subconscious mind remembers the past and our imaginative mind conjures the future, so our conscious mind exists only in the moment we call now. Key 2 represents our past, memory, and subconscious mind. Key 3 represents our probable future, our imagined future, our imagination or our imaginative mind. Key Four represents our conscious mind.

The span of time we call now is very small compared to our past and our future. Now is only a few seconds at a time. The past is all of life we've lived to this moment. Our memory also contains the history of other times, places, events, and people. So our subconscious mind is very large. They say that if our unconscious mind were a basketball our subconscious mind would be a baseball and our conscious mind a pea. Our imaginative mind can be very small or very large depending upon how much we use it. The more we imagine the possibilities, the larger and more active this mind becomes. While our subconscious mind continues to grow in size as we learn more and more, and our imaginative mind grows in size the more we use it, our conscious mind does not grow in size.

The true power of our conscious mind is not its size but its ability to tap into our past and into our future. The knowledge of our past and the knowledge we've learned along the way are all available to our conscious mind when we make a decision. The dreams and aspirations of our future are also available to our conscious mind when we make a decision. Even with all that power we can still make mistakes.

That power is under our control. We decide how much we want to rely on the lessons of the past and our plans for the future. We can ignore past lessons and future probabilities or we can act on them. The decision is ours.

They say "To err is human." My interpretation of this is we all make mistakes because our reasoning power is impaired. Through no fault of our own we often do not have all the facts necessary to make a correct decision. Through no fault of our own some of the facts we have are incorrect and decisions based on incorrect facts are wrong decisions no matter what alibis we may use. Through no fault of our own we may make the right decision but the end result is wrong.

The rational person, the one who reasons things out, who thinks things through, accepts the inevitability of making mistakes from time to time. The rational person makes the best decisions he or she can make at the time. The rational person then makes more decisions as necessary in order to move ahead and get on with his or her life. The rational person accepts mistakes as only mistakes and learns from the experience.

The irrational person does not accept making mistakes as being the normal human condition. The irrational person either doesn't make any decisions or waits for somebody else to make them. In the meantime, the irrational person acts on impulse or relies on his or her unconscious instincts to solve any problems. The irrational person thinks mistakes are a flaw in his or her personality. Mistakes are not personality flaws. They are merely mistakes.

Universal Law Four is represented by Key 4, the Emperor who thinks for him or herself. If we apply the Fourth Universal Law to Key 4, we arrive at the following keywords, phrases and/or concepts:

- Reason it out for yourself
- Make your own decisions
- Accept your mistakes and move on
- Decide what you want your spiritual life to be like
- Decide how you want to behave
- Reason out your intentions
- Decide which attitudes you want to express
- Make a decision

If you'd like to go one step further, assign the pip card fours to have the same meaning as Universal Law Four except the meaning applies to the elements rather than your spiritual path.

The Fourth Universal Law is important because it forms the basis of who and what you are right now.

5

Universal Law Five says everybody has intuition and anybody can develop his or her intuitive mind. It's a matter of choice. We can develop our intuitive faculties if we wish to do so. We can also choose not to do so. But even then, our intuitive mind may speak to us from time to time.

Let's review the minds we've discussed so far:

- Unconscious Mind which controls our automatic systems (Key 1)
- Subconscious Mind which is our memory of the past (Key 2)
- Imaginative Mind which is our expectations for the future (Key 3)
- Rational Mind which is our thinking mind (in the present) (Key 4)

These four minds are chatterboxes. The Corporeal Mind, which is part of our Unconscious Mind, is forever telling us we need something to make the body happy: "Feed me. Give me a drink. Move this body part. Relax. Scratch here."

Our Subconscious Mind reminds us all the time about what we did sometime in our past in a similar situation. It takes control and helps us react the same way again. Whenever the opportunity arises to remind us of something, our subconscious mind will grab the chance to do just that. It's amazing what it remembers.

Our Imaginative Mind incessantly tells us what we might be able to do regardless of reality at the moment. Whenever a thought comes into our mind, our Imagination conjures up possibility after possibility whether these options are reasonable or not.

Our Rational Mind is caught in the middle trying to make sense out of all these other thoughts and reason everything out. It works in our dreams, keeps us awake at night and tires us out during the day. It never stops thinking about something.

It's a wonder with all this going on we never get anything done. We get things done by focusing our thoughts and ideas. We focus our thoughts and ideas by using two tools: (1) Intention and (2) Attitude.

Our Intention controls who and what we are. We can only do those things we intend to do. We can only become what we intend to become. We are today exactly what we intended to be at this time and in this place. Our memories are of the things we intended to do.

When a person says "I didn't mean to do that" or "I didn't intend to do that," what it means is "On a conscious level that was not my intention." In other words, on a subconscious or unconscious level he or she did intend to do such and such.

These four minds we've been discussing work on the conscious, unconscious, and subconscious levels all the time. They work on tirelessly whether we're in charge or not. If we're not in charge, one of them is. If we get stuck in our conscious mind we ruminate about everything and do nothing. Our mind goes round and round and we can't make a decision. We procrastinate. Things don't get done. Things get worse and as they get worse we worry about them more and more. Eventually, we hide in our subconscious or imaginative minds.

If we get stuck in our subconscious mind we remember everything whether we want to remember it right now or not. One past event after another parades before our eyes reminding us of all our past wrongs. We were wronged or we caused harm. The longer we stay in this state the more prone we are to depression, anger, and guilt.

If we get stuck in our imaginative mind we conjure up every possible outcome whether based on reality or not. We imagine everything that can go wrong, every way we can get hurt. The longer we stay in this state the more prone we are to anxiety, anger, and mania.

If we get stuck in our unconscious mind we can lose touch with reality and wander through the recesses of our mind or we can become obsessive about our body. The more we obsess about our body the more prone we are to illness and physical or mental disorders. We become what we worry we might become.

Not a pretty picture, but this is what happens if we do not take control of our own lives. We take control by our Intention. What we intend to do is what our minds all want to help us do. But if we do not give our minds this direction they have no choice but to do something based on what they think our intention might be.

We can understand what our minds think our intention is for our life by examining our own thoughts. Whatever we think is what our minds think is our intention for our life. Therefore, whatever we think is what we will become.

To change what you will be in the future all you need to change is your intention. Your intention for your own future is determined by the goals you set for yourself on a daily, weekly, monthly, yearly, and lifetime basis. Change these goals and you change who and what you will become.

Here's the problem: You have goals for yourself whether you know it or not. It's the goals you don't even know about that run your life and change you into what you will become. Decide what you want to become and make a conscious decision to intend to become that person.

Yes, your intention is a conscious decision. You can decide what you want to do and become. This is your intention. Or you can let things be as they are and your minds will make that decision for you consciously, subconsciously, or unconsciously.

Your minds will make that decision based on your attitude or on what they perceive your attitude to have been or what it might become or what it is right now. Attitude is everything. It controls what your minds think you are now, were in the past, or will be in the future. Attitude, like intention, is a decision. You can decide to be happy or dejected, cheerful or sad, optimistic or pessimistic, laughing or crying, playful or rigid. Once you decide, your mind accept this as your attitude until you change it.

As a tarot reader, one of your more difficult tasks will be to teach your clients that they get to choose how they handle adversity. Life is hard. We all get hurt. We are all wronged. Bad things happen to all of us. But through it all, we get to choose what our attitude will be and we get to choose our intentions for our own life. That's the lesson of the first four minds.

The lesson of our fifth mind, our intuitive mind, is that we can hear the small quiet voice of our own intuition when we quiet down all the other voices. Like them, it's always awake, always working, always on the job. When we don't hear our intuition it's because we're not listening or because some other louder sound is overriding it. The key to this is knowing what the other minds are doing (we just reviewed that) and how to quiet them down.

Universal Law Five says everybody has intuition and anybody can develop his or her intuitive mind. It's a matter of choice. We can develop our intuitive faculties if we wish to do so. We can also choose not to do so. But even then, our intuitive mind may speak to us from time to time.

Our intuition speaks to us in a small quiet unobtrusive voice. If your inner voice shouts at you or talks over your other thoughts, you can be assured this is your subconscious mind, imagination, or conscious mind speaking to you and not your intuition. Even when whispering so silently you can barely hear them, your conscious, subconscious, and imaginative minds always speak louder than your intuitive mind. Your intuition really is a small, quiet voice within.

Our intuitive mind never makes any demands of us in any way. It never tells us what to do. If your inner voice is telling you what to do, you can rest assured it's not your intuition speaking. It may be your conscious, subconscious, or imaginative mind, but it's definitely not your intuition.

When we're thinking with our normal conscious or rational mind, we're aware these thoughts are in our heads. Our memories and thoughts of the future (subconscious and imaginative minds) also seem to be centered in our heads most of the time. Sometimes we have the feeling that our memories and thoughts are out there somewhere and not really within us.

Our intuitive mind rarely gives us the impression it's speaking inside our heads. We might hear sounds but we know the sound is not coming through our ears. We may see visions but we know these sights are not coming through our eyes. We may feel sensations, taste, or smell things but we know these things are not being sensed by our skin, tongue, or nose.

Our intuitive mind generally gives us the impression it's coming from deep within ourselves. It's like our skin in the outside peel of an onion and we reside within that onion. Deep at the center of the onion is our intuition. Everything else is closer to the surface.

Our intuitive mind is beyond emotion and never makes us feel emotional about anything. If the voice you hear is filled with anger, hate, or fear, you can rest assured it's not your intuition. If the voice you hear is filled with unconditional love and acceptance in an nonemotional way, you're probably listening to your inner voice, your intuition.

Since the intuitive mind speaks with such a soft and quiet voice, you must quiet down the other voices in order to hear it. One way to quiet these other minds down is to use Keys 1–4 to help you. It works like this:

Key 1—Quiet down the unconscious mind. We do this by sitting quietly and consciously relaxing our muscles. We breathe deeply and as we breathe, we relax. By practicing this for as little as five minutes a day you can learn to almost instantly quiet down your unconscious mind.

Key 2—Quiet down the subconscious mind. We do this by dismissing any memories about anything that come into our consciousness. We dismiss these memories by telling these memories you'll consider them later but not now. With very little practice your subconscious mind will stop the flow of memories whenever you become calm and breathe deeply. The subconscious mind always does what it thinks we want it to do.

Key 3—Quiet down the imagination. We do this by dismissing any future possibilities that come into our consciousness. We do this by telling these fantasies we'll consider them later but not now. Our imaginative mind seems to be very influenced by our subconscious mind, so it usually quiets down too.

Key 4—Quiet down our conscious mind. We do this by dismissing any thoughts that come into our consciousness. We do this by telling these thoughts we'll consider them later but not now.

Throughout this process, we continue to breathe deeply and relax our muscles while remaining in a comfortable and alert state of mind and body. When you do this you'll be surprised to hear your own small, quiet, unobtrusive, calming, and peaceful inner voice. Listen and be at peace.

Pose a question to your inner voice and wait for the answer. Keep breathing deeply, stay relaxed and alert. Expect answers and you'll receive them. The more you practice this technique the easier it will be for you to tune into your own intuitive mind.

We said earlier that our subconscious mind is infallible, it remembers everything perfectly, even the lies we tell it and ourselves. We also said our conscious mind is subject to error and is not infallible. Our imagination does not remember things and it does not make any decisions. It projects future possibilities for us and we can attain some of these possibilities. But sometimes our imaginations run away with us and we dream impossible dreams.

Our intuitive mind, being the small quiet voice it is, can be dominated by any of our other minds if we allow that to happen. They'd all like to get into the act every time you ask your intuition a question. Our unconscious mind will keep us very busy satisfying the needs of the body if we let it. We quiet it down by relaxing, breathing deeply, and not paying any attention to its incessant requests for this or that.

Our subconscious mind would like to share memories with us. Tell it thank you very much, we'll consider these things later, but just now we're talking with our intuition and we'd appreciate it if there were no more interruptions. Thank you.

Our conscious, rational, mind would like to figure it all out, reason it through. Our imagination would like to take these ideas and run with them. We quiet them both down in the same loving manner we used to set our subconscious mind aside for the time being and we listen to our intuition.

Universal Law Five is represented by Key 5, the Hierophant who intuits everything. If we apply the Fifth Universal Law to Key 5, we arrive at the following keywords, phrases, and/or concepts:

- Expect and anticipate intuitive insights
- Become still and know the truth from within
- Discover that peace within
- Trust your gut feelings
- Do it only if it "feels" right

If you'd like to go one step further, assign the pip card fives to have the same meaning as Universal Law Five except the meaning applies to the elements rather than your spiritual path.

The Fifth Universal Law is important because it helps you communicate with the true you, your own spiritual self.

6

Universal Law Six indicates we have the right of self-determination, we have free will to do what we want to do and to become what we want to become. More than this, we have a conscience to help us decide what's right and what's wrong. But our conscience only helps us by telling us what's right and what's wrong. The decision to do or not to do is ours and that's where our free will comes in.

Our conscience helps us by discriminating between this and that, telling us what each thing is and whether it's right or wrong to become involved with each thing. What a powerful tool this is and isn't it too bad most of us pay little attention to our conscience from time to time?

Our conscience tells us if our ideas come from the past (where they're stored in our subconscious mind), the future (where they're a figment of our imaginative mind), or the present (where they're actively being considered by our rational mind). Our conscience tells us if we need to pay attention to our bodily needs (which are under the supervision of our unconscious mind) or if we're receiving intuitive insights from our own higher self (our intuitive mind).

Our conscience discriminates between all these minds and evaluates the "goodness" or "badness" of each item coming from each mind. Our conscience is infallible in performing its duty. It's up to us to do the right thing or not. Any error in judgment is ours and ours alone.

Universal Law Six is represented by the Lovers who represent our conscious (masculine) mind, our subconscious (feminine) mind, and our own higher self (our intuitive mind). The state of nakedness is a reminder of our unconscious mind and the Trees of Knowledge and Life remind us of our imaginative minds.

Universal Law Six asks us to use our powers of discrimination and discernment to ascertain the rightness or wrongness of a planned reaction (masculine), interaction (feminine), or event (neutral). It asks us to tell the difference between things, events, people, or our own minds.

If we apply the Sixth Universal Law to Key 6, we arrive at the following keywords, phrases, and/or concepts:

- Discriminate
- Tell the difference (between this and that)
- Decide what's right and what's not (at least for you)
- Be certain that's really what you want to do
- Be certain that's really the relationship you want
- Ascertain where this idea is coming from in your head
- Let your conscience be your guide

If you'd like to go one step further, assign the pip card sixes to have the same meaning as Universal Law Six except the meaning applies to the elements rather than your spiritual path.

The Sixth Universal Law is important because it defines our conscience.

7

Universal Law Seven says you have a right to receive Divine Grace, Divine Love, Divine Blessings, and Divine Intervention in your life, and Communication with the Divine (Communion).

You don't have to be religious. You don't have to belong to any particular religion. You don't even have to be spiritual. You're entitled to receive these things any time you ask. You can call upon the Divine any time, by any name, in any language, in prayer, meditation, by ritual or in supplication and you can expect the Divine to respond.

You may not receive the response you want, but the Divine will respond. You may not receive your response as quickly as you might like, but you will receive it. This is your God-given right.

You don't have a right to demand, you have a right to ask. You don't have a right to be abusive; you have an obligation to be loving and respectful. You also have the right to be treated lovingly and respectfully.

Your receptive mind is your gateway to the Divine. This mind is between your conscience and your Creator. Some even say our conscience acts as a link in the communications which come from our Creator to our conscience, to our intuitive mind, and on down through our rational mind, imaginative mind, subconscious mind to our brain (our attentive mind).

The problem as they see it is that every mind in between the Creator and your brain gets into the act and "rearranges the message," so to speak. Each one of them adds a bit of advice or what appears to be a useful comment.

So how can you tune in directly with your receptive mind? The secret is first to tune into your intuition as we discussed in Universal Law Five. As this communication deepens you'll start to receive impressions that something is good or bad, right or wrong. Good. Your conscience is speaking to you and you hear the message. Great!

Now all you have to do is advise your conscience that you receive the message and you appreciate it. Now please calm down so we both can hear directly from the Divine. You may not hear anything right away, or for some time really. But you will start to feel Divine Love fill your entire being. Keep breathing deeply, relaxing your minds and body, and letting go of all tensions and thoughts. Let the Divine Love infuse your being.

This is what the yogis call Bliss. This feeling of unconditional love intensifies with practice and you receive Divine Grace, Divine Love, Divine Blessing, and you know the Divine is intervening in your life. Nobody tells you this, you just know. Eventually, you'll hear a very quiet voice coming from deep inside you (you may even think it's coming from your heart) and the voice will tell you "I Love You" and you'll believe the Divine does love you.

You've just received your first message from the Divine. Now you know how to attain this receptive state. With practice you can attain it more and more quickly and sustain it for a longer and longer period of time.

Universal Law Seven says you have:

- a right to receive Divine Grace
- a right to receive Divine Love
- a right to receive Divine Blessings
- a right to receive Divine Intervention
- a right to communicate with the Divine

Your receptive mind is exemplified by the Chariot. Universal Law Seven is represented by the Chariot. The Chariot asks us to use our receptive mind to become receptive to Divine Influences and Communication in our life. The sevens in the pip cards ask us to do the same thing with regard to the element of the card.

Each of the Seven Universal Laws we've discussed so far is related to one of our seven minds. The next Seven Universal Laws are related to the lessons each of us learns during our lifetime. Now's a good time to go back and review the First through the Seventh Universal Laws.

8

Universal Law Eight says you have the strength to take control of your own life. This is the first of the Seven Great Lessons we must learn during our lifetime.

If you happen to be using a deck where Key 8 is Justice or something similar to Justice, you'll need to use Key 11 for this particular Universal Law. The older tradition had its reasons to assign Justice to position 8 and place Strength in the middle of the Major Arcana. But we won't go there.

If you happen to be studying tarot with one of the mystery school traditions, you'll learn your subconscious mind likes to do what you want it to do. In fact, whatever you tell your subconscious mind, it will attempt to do. If you tell your subconscious mind you're fat, your subconscious mind will do everything in its power to make you fat. If you tell your subconscious mind you can't do something, your subconscious mind will do everything possible to make sure you can't do that thing. This is the power of suggestion.

Suggestion is what some mystery schools name this card. The idea is that whatever you tell your subconscious mind to see as true and real and will become your reality. If you say I am (blank) you will become (blank) because your subconscious mind will do everything it can to make (blank) become a reality in your life, even if what you tell your subconscious mind is a little white lie.

Your subconscious mind knows imagination is just that, but it doesn't know properly done affirmations, visualizations, and prayers are little white lies. So it does everything possible to make the content of these little white lies happen to you. That's not how the mystics would explain it, but that's how it is. It works like this:

- Decide what change you want to make in your life
- Write it down in detail
- Compose an affirmation stated in the present tense
- Create a visualization of the desired result happening now
- Use your affirmation and visualization as a prayer

Decide what change you want to make in your life. Be very specific. The more specific the change you want to make, the better your chances are of obtaining that change. The more general you are, the less specific the changes are. For example, if your goal is to lose weight, you can spend a lot of time visualizing, affirming, and praying for a few ounces of weight loss. But, if you put the same amount of energy into affirming, visualizing, and praying for a specific weight, you'll achieve your goal.

Both ways you achieve your goal. The second way is better because your subconscious mind knows exactly what to do to help you become who you claim to be. The first way works if you want to get fat. The more you think you're fat, the fatter you become.

Write it all down in your journal or diary and date your entry. There's something about the process of writing something down that gives us ownership. Until we write it down, it's just a pipe dream (some say it's a nightmare).

Compose your goal in an affirmation stated in the present tense. Just state what it is you want to achieve and use a present-tense verb. State your affirmation as a goal already achieved. That's the secret of suggestion. That's the secret of taking control of your own life. That's what you, the person in the strength card, do to your subconscious mind, the red lion. You take control through the power of suggestion.

Use this affirmation to create a visualization of already having attained this goal. Visualize yourself, not as you are now, but as you see yourself when your goal is achieved. The secret is to see yourself as though your goal were already achieved. See yourself doing whatever it is you stated in your goal. Visualize yourself being exactly what you want to be, doing exactly what you want to do, and tell your subconscious mind a little white lie. Your subconscious mind will believe you and do everything it can do to make your thoughts become your reality. That's what your subconscious mind does, it makes your thoughts your reality.

What you think today is what you will be tomorrow. Your very own subconscious mind will make that happen whether you like it or not. Take control of your life and you will be tomorrow what you want to be.

Finally, *use your affirmation and visualization as a prayer.* Ask for Divine intervention. It's very simple. One possible masculine weight-loss prayer is "Dear Father–Mother–Creator God help me to weigh 200 lbs of firm muscle, bone and skin." Visualize this. Affirm this. Attain this.

Beware. Suggestion works. Whatever you suggest to your subconscious mind will come to pass. If you think you're fat, you'll be fat or fatter. If you think you can't, you can't and you never will. Like the little train going up the mountain, if you think you can you will, because you always become tomorrow what you think today.

That's Universal Law Eight. The Strength card tells you to take control of your own life and to become what you want to become. You'll either become the person of your wildest dreams or your worst nightmares. Control your thoughts and you control who you are.

This same principle can be applied to the eights in the Minor Arcana according to the elements.

9

Universal Law Nine says you have the right to receive Divine love, influence, and grace in your life. This is the second of the Seven Great Lessons we must learn in this lifetime.

The truth is we can't survive in this world of pain and suffering without Divine grace, love, guidance, and influence in our lives. Therefore we must have asked for and received some Divine influence in our lives already.

Notice this law says we have the right to receive this grace. This right is optional at our choice. We can choose to receive Divine love, grace, intervention, influence, or guidance. The choice is ours to make each and every day of our lives, each and every moment of our lives.

We receive this Divine love, grace, intervention, influence, guidance, ministering, and intercession by simply asking for it. Until we ask, we're not exercising our right to receive. By asking we become receptive and we open ourselves to receiving. Until we ask, we're not receptive, we're not exercising our right to receive.

There are two important things you need to know about this Law in order to be able to exercise your Divine right. First of all, this law does not say to ask for Divine help and do nothing. This is not a law intended to make you lazy. You must continue to work for everything you want to manifest in your life. That's why you're here in the first place, to work for what you receive.

Because we're responsible for our own lives, because we need to work in this lifetime, and because this world is not a nice place for everybody all the time, some theologians call this place Hell. They may be right. But in my opinion, we make this place a living hell ourselves by our thoughts, words, and deeds.

The rest of the story is we can make this a pleasant place to live and work by our thoughts, words, and deeds. If we're living in Hell today, we can reside in Heaven tomorrow. We do that by changing our thoughts, words, and deeds and by receiving Divine love, grace, intercession, interaction, guidance, influence, and ministering in our lives.

Secondly, we must actively become receptive, we must open our receptive mind to the Divine. We learned how to do that in the last phase of our childhood and it depended upon all the preceding steps as we learned in Keys 1 through 6. In short, we must:

- Calm and relax our body
- Calm and set aside our memories
- Calm and set aside our imagination
- Calm and set aside our thinking mind
- Open our intuitive mind and quiet it down
- Quiet our conscience and use it as a channel
- Become receptive to the Divine

In Key 8 we learned to use our Strength to change our lives through the power of suggestion using Affirmations and Visualizations. Now we learn the power of Prayer. We learn to ask and keep on working with the expectation of receiving Divine intervention, influence, grace, intercession, ministering, love, and interaction. We ask and we receive. We knock and it is opened to us.

We communicate with the Divine in thought, word, and deed through prayer, ritual, and meditation just as we communicate with our own Higher Self and subconscious mind through suggestions, affirmations, and visualizations. We can combine the two and our Strength becomes even greater.

Key 9 exemplifies this Universal Law. The Hermit holds up the Light of the World for us to see our way in this dark world. If we but ask in prayer for assistance, the light becomes brighter and our path is easier to travel.

Every religion known to me teaches this great lesson. It's the second of the Seven Great Secrets we must learn during our lifetime. Universal Law Nine says no matter what you do, you're an example for other people who choose to learn from you.

That's a powerful lesson to learn in life. No matter what we do, some people are going to look up to us and follow our lead. Some people are going to see what we do, hear what we say and get inside our heads to do, speak and think the same things we're doing, speaking and thinking.

That's awesome. It's also scary. Some people are going to say the same things we probably shouldn't have said. Some people are going to do the same things we probably shouldn't have done. Some people are going to think the same things we probably would have been better off not thinking about. Some people are going to use us as their role model, their mentor, or their teacher. They probably won't even ask us if they can, they'll just do it.

That's really scary. Some people are going to make the same mistakes in life we made because they're going to copy us. And what makes it really worrisome is we may not even know they're doing it. Some people are going to imitate what we do, say and think, and we won't even know it. We're a role model for other people whether we know it or not.

That's an awesome responsibility, being a role model. The more you think about it, the more cause you have to be concerned about what you do, say, and think. Imagine the trouble some people are going to have in this life because they do, say, and think like us. It boggles the imagination to even consider all the ramifications.

This is the second of the Seven Great Lessons we need to learn in this lifetime. The lesson comes in two parts: (1) the realization some other people would even want to be like us, and (2) the realization this places a tremendous responsibility upon us to do, speak, and think only beneficial things in this life.

We look at our lives and wonder why people would ever want to use us as a mentor. Then we look around to the people who taught us something we consider to be useful in life. They taught us this by their actions, words, and thoughts. They may not even know we learned something from them. They may not even know we do, say, or think certain things because we admire that in them.

Then we realize other people might be using us in the same way. We taught them something by our thoughts, words, and deeds and we didn't even know it. They might not even know it.

Life's like that. We go around teaching, modeling, and mentoring each other all the time whether we know it or not. Universal Law Nine brings this to our attention.

Now we get to choose how we think, speak, and act knowing other people will learn these things from us. What role model do we want to portray? What things do we want to teach? What image do we want to portray? What about us do we want others to copy? How do we want to be a mentor in this life?

Key 9 exemplifies Universal Law Nine. The Hermit stands on the heights he or she has attained and holds up his or her light for others to follow. The Hermit is you and I whether we want to be the Hermit or not. That's the message and lesson we need to learn from Universal Law Nine.

The first lesson was that we are today what we suggested to ourselves we would become yesterday. We are the result of our thoughts. Our lives are the result of our thoughts, words, and deeds. The rest of the lesson is that we can become tomorrow what we suggest to ourselves we are today.

The second lesson is no matter who and what we are, other people are learning from us how to speak, think, and act. We are mentors, role models, and teachers whether we want to be or not. The rest of the lesson is for each of us to guide ourselves accordingly.

Having learned this lesson, we have an obligation to everybody in the world to become a better person that we already are. We have an obligation to watch and control our thoughts and our speech and our actions for the highest good of everybody. More than that, we have an obligation to all other people to become a spiritual person, to improve ourselves, to be the best we can be, and to act, speak, and think only for the good of everybody.

That's what Universal Law Nine and the Hermit communicate to us. That's also the message of the nines in the Minor Arcana as it applies to the element of the suit involved.

10

Universal Law Ten says what goes around, comes around; what you do to others in intention, feeling, thought, word, or deed, happens to you. What you intend to do to others happens to you. What you feel you want to do to others happens to you. What you think you want to do to others happens to you. What you speak about doing to others happens to you. What you do to others also happens to you.

It's the original Golden Rule which says what you think, speak, and do for good will always manifest good in this world. But what you do, speak, and think about doing to cause harm to another, brings harm upon you. We help ourselves by helping others and we harm ourselves by attempting to harm others.

This is the Law of Cause and Effect. It means we cause our own pain and suffering in this world. Other people may cause us harm, but we cause our own pain and suffering. We do this by our attitude regarding any harm or negativity that comes our way. With a strong positive attitude, we can overcome anything. With a negative attitude, we cause ourselves pain and suffering.

The message is that we reap what we sow. If we go about trying to hurt other people, we end up hurting ourselves. If we go about tearing other people down, we ruin our own reputation. If we sow negativity, we reap negativity in our lives.

Universal Law Ten is represented by Key 10, The Wheel of Fortune, and the tens of the Minor Arcana.

11

Universal Law Eleven says that everything's the way it's supposed to be.

When we look at the world and see it as being unfair and capricious, we see an illusion. The reality is that the world is undeviatingly just in all things all the time. When "bad" things happen to us, it's because something neutral happened and we perceive it as being "bad." How we react to that something makes all the difference in who and what we are. The event itself is meaningless no matter how "bad" we perceive it to be. It's our attitude that makes all the difference.

This is the hardest Universal Law for most of us to accept. It's easy for us to blame other people, events, things, even God for the negative things that happen to us. The truth is that some bad things just happen and nobody is to "blame."

When we can't find anybody or anything else to blame, it's easy to blame ourselves for the negative things that happen to us. The truth is that some things just happen and we're not to blame either.

Our problem comes in trying to reconcile Universal Laws Ten and Eleven. When we attempt to harm another, it's difficult for us to accept the harm we cause ourselves as having been caused by us. We tend to blame anyone and anything for our discomfort. When some random event causes us harm, it's easy for us to blame ourselves because we perceive ourselves as being "bad."

The truth is that we can cause ourselves harm by attempting to harm others. The truth is that this is a world of pain and suffering and there are times when things happen over which we have no control. The solution to our pain and suffering is to intend, think, feel, speak and do good things for others, and to forgive ourselves when we don't.

We also need to be prepared to forgive others when they fail to intend, think, feel, speak, and do good things for us or others too. That's part of doing good deeds.

The rest of the solution is to maintain a positive attitude and belief in God no matter what. If we truly believe there is some good in all people and all things, we need to concentrate on that good. The bad we turn over to God as we understand Him or Her.

This world and everything in it is exactly the way it's supposed to be. Injustice and justice exist for a purpose whether we understand it or not, and whether we believe it or not. Good and evil, nice and bad, all opposites exist for reasons whether we understand them or not, and whether we believe them or not. Everything in this world is just exactly the way it's supposed to be.

There's one partial exception to this rule and that exception is you and I. We're exactly who and what we want to be and we have the power and authority to change that any time we want. This is the true meaning of "Free Will." We have the free will to change who and what we are, at any time, and that's also the way that it's supposed to be.

Universal Law Eleven is represented by Key 11 and the Pages of the Minor Arcana.

12

Universal Law Twelve tells us to reverse our thinking. We believe this physical universe is our existence. We need to reverse our thinking. We believe we're victims and other people are the cause of our problems. We need to reverse our thinking. We believe the events in our lives are the cause of our difficulties. We need to reverse our thinking.

We need to reverse our thinking and truly understand the message of Universal Laws Ten and Eleven. These Universal Laws teach us that we're the result of our previous intentions, thoughts, feelings, words, and actions. We are today exactly the persons our previous intentions, thoughts, feelings, words, and acts created us to be. We're not perfect. We're flawed and we created that flawed person.

Universal Law Twelve tells us to reverse our thinking. This Universal Law tells us that first and foremost we're spiritual beings. By our thoughts, words, and deeds, most of us deny this great truth. We need to reverse our thinking. We think the events of this life are more important than anything. We need to reverse our thinking.

Key 12 and the Knights are representations of this Law. Key 12 advises us to reverse our thinking about our spiritual self. The Knights advise us to reverse our thinking about whatever their element means to you.

Notice that Universal Law Twelve does not say anything about blaming ourselves for who and what we are. It says to forget the blame and change our thinking.

13

Universal Law Thirteen tells us to change our behavior. Before we can change our behavior, we need to change our thinking about ourselves, our life, and our purpose for living. Key 12 sends us that message.

Once we change our thinking, we're ready to change our behavior. In all things, thought comes before action. We decide we don't like being prejudiced against something or somebody, some group or some person. Once we make that decision and change our thinking (Key 12), we're ready to change our behavior (Key 13), to become a better person.

We'll always react to the same or similar situations the same way we've always reacted until we change our thinking. Then we can make a rational decision to change our behavior. Just because we change our thinking doesn't mean we change our behavior. That's why Universal Law Thirteen exists.

Changing our thinking is a requirement for changing our behavior. Once we do change our thinking we need next to analyze our previous behavior and then decide what we're going to change and how. Then we need to make the change.

Changing behavior requires repetition. It's easy to revert to our old way of doing things because our old ways were habits. We'd done the same thing so many times it became automatic for us. Changing behavior requires we do the new thing so many times tillthat it becomes a new habit which can that replaces the old.

That's where affirmations and visualizations come in. We can use these tools to help us change our behavior. We can also use prayer, meditations, and rituals for this purpose. We can use twelve-step programs and other self-help approaches to change our behavior.

Here's one interesting way of looking at the tools we can use to change our behavior:

Key 1—Rituals (using our magickal implements = our body)
Key 2—Prayer (using our subconsciousmind)
Key 3—Visualizations (using our imagination)
Key 4—Affirmations (using our rational mind)
Key 5—Meditation (using our intuition)
Key 6—Group therapy (using our conscience)
Key 7—Divine intervention (using our receptive mind)
Key 13—Universal Law Thirteen which tells us to change our
    spiritual behavior.

The Queens tell us to change our behavior in the areas represented by the meanings you assign to their suits. The Pages tell us everything's the way it's supposed to be regarding their suit. The Knights tell us to change our thinking about the things represented by their suits. In the next lesson we'll learn that the Kings speak to us about verifying that what we have represented by their suit is what we want.

Isn't this an interesting way of looking at the court cards? It's all part of the mystical system for learning how to read tarot cards. You can also use numerological or astrological systems to handle the court cards in a similar manner. In these systems the court cards represent recommendations, suggestions, and advice rather than people. It's an interesting approach.

14

Now is a good time to review the previous thirteen Universal Laws. The Fourteenth Universal Law requires us to review everything we've done in order to decide if that's what we really want.

Universal Law Fourteen asks us to verify that who and what we are is who and what we really want to be. It also asks us to verify that the people and things in our life are the people and things we really want in our lives. It asks us to take a good look at ourselves and make sure we're doing what we want to be doing with our life. That's the Law of Verification.

You may find this strange, but in a recent survey done by a large corporation, only sixteen percent of the employees indicated they were doing the job they wanted to be doing. Eighty-four percent of their employees were doing a job they didn't really want to do. Even more startling was the fact that forty-one percent didn't even want to be working for that company. The results were fairly consistent across ranks. Entry-level employees scored no worse than upper-level employees. Management was rightfully concerned.

You may think that this speaks poorly of the company. My reaction is that it speaks poorly of the employees. My question is "Why would anyone work in a job they didn't like?"

Money.

What other reason could there be? People don't usually go around doing things they don't want to do. People don't usually like to do things they don't want to do. Why suffer through a job you didn't like except for the money?

The Law of Verification would help these people identify that their lives are not the way they want them to be. It would help them to see they are not who they want to be. It might help them see that money may not be worth the sacrifice.

Who and what should we be? That's the question we need to answer. It's a decision we need to make. Once we make that decision we use our Spiritual Strength (Key Eight) to become that person. Then we let our Light shine so others may follow our example (Key 9). We resolve the conflicts in our life by doing to others what we'd like to happen to us (Key 10). We treat every other person and thing as fairly as we can and realize everything is as it should be (Key 11). We change our thinking (Key 12) and we change our behavior (Key 13). We become new and different persons and we verify that's what we want (Key 14). That's who and what we should be, who and what we want to be.

When we start to verify we're doing exactly what we want to be doing, we'll probably discover we're not. We've fallen short. That means we go back to universal Law Eight and work our way up to Law Fourteen over and over until we're doing what we want to be doing.

What should we do? We should first of all do what we love to do. Secondly, we should do something which expresses who and what we are. Thirdly, we should do what we really want to do to help ourselves and all others. Note we should not do what we want to do at the expense of ourselves or others. That's the process of verification.

Verification is represented by Key 14 and the four Kings. Temperance asks us to verify that we are spiritually who and what we want to be.

The Kings ask us to verify we are who and what we want to be, doing what we want to do with respect to the things defined by the Elements the Kings represent. Define the Elements and you know what each King is asking you to verify.

If you've been following this discussion and applying the results to your tarot deck, you've defined seventy cards in your deck. You've defined fourteen cards of the Major Arcana, sixteen court cards, and forty pip cards. Only eight more cards to go. That's the way life is. Once you reach the point where you verify that you are who and what you want to be, doing the things you want to do, the mundane life is behind you. You're ready to spiritually advance beyond your fondest dreams. We'll start that journey in the next lesson.

15

We now start the last leg of our spiritual journey.

The first seven Universal Laws identified our seven minds and challenged us to use them for the good of all. The next seven laws outlined our duty, our responsibility to ourselves and all others, in this lifetime. Now's a good time to go back and review the first fourteen Universal Laws in this light.

Universal Law Fifteen says you need to quit the darkness and seek the light. You need to overcome your ignorance and become knowledgeable. Knowledge is light. Ignorance is darkness.

We live in ignorance when we harm others in thought, word, or deed. We live in ignorance when we harm ourselves in thought, word, or deed. The words we speak, the acts we do, and the ideas we think all reveal our ignorance. We live in ignorance when we fail to love unconditionally.

Love is a decision. We express our love by our thoughts, our words, and our acts We express our lack of unconditional love by our thoughts, words, and acts. We express our ignorance daily, sometimes hourly. By the things we do, the things we say, and the things we think we express our lack of unconditional love. We live in darkness.

We are ignorant. Ignorant of what? We're ignorant of who and what we really are. We're ignorant of our spiritual self, our capacity to love unconditionally.

Look around you. Most people live in darkness. We're like sheep milling around, running away from this and that. We don't understand our potential and we don't remember our duty. We don't know our purpose. We don't acknowledge our talents, and sometimes we hide them or even deny them.

We harm each other by our words and our thoughts. We harm each other by our intentions and our feelings toward them. We hurt and violate each other. We call this "the human condition" and thereby prove our ignorance and our inability to love unconditionally. Who among us doesn't wish harm to those who caused our great suffering on September 11th? This is an example of our ignorance. True, those who perpetrated this great disaster were also ignorant and they caused us all great harm. Is this an excuse to wish them harm? That's a question we must all as ourselves as we seek to discover the truth about life and ourselves.

We acknowledge our own ignorance with any affirmative answer of any kind. The more harm we wish them, the greater the darkness in our life, the deeper our ignorance. That's what Key 15 is all about, to remind us we live in darkness, that we're ignorant. If we know that much, we have the ability to light the lamp of knowledge. There is hope for us. We can learn to love and love unconditionally.

16

As we move out of the darkness toward the light, we occasionally have a flash of lightning to illumine our way. As we move out of the darkness of our ignorance, we occasionally have a flash of inspiration that adds to our knowledge.

As we move from Key 15 to Key 16 we make this transition from absolute ignorance to an occasional insight. We're no longer mired down in absolute ignorance but we have very little knowledge. This reminds me of the sightless grub moving through the transformation to sight in a new body.

In the first stages of this new body, the grub has occasional glimpses of light. As the stages progress so does the sense of sight improve until finally a new creature emerges into the light.

This is the process we go through as we move from Key 15 to Key 21 step by step, key by key. We move from absolute ignorance to absolute knowledge. We move from absolute darkness to perfect light, step by step.

Universal Law Sixteen tells us to awaken to the reality of the truth about ourselves. We're spiritual creatures filled with perfect knowledge but we don't believe that. We're spiritual creatures of pure white light but we don't believe that. Maybe we're just beginning to believe that light and knowledge just might be part of the truth of life. Every once in a while we get a glimpse of reality but we aren't quite sure what we saw wasn't an illusion. We doubt ourselves.

As we go through this process, in the darkness of our mind, we eventually reach a point where one last flash of insight does the trick. One last glimpse of reality awakens us to the fact we've been living in ignorance. This awakening can come in an instant or over a long period of time, but when it comes we know there is more to life than what we see. We know that beyond any shadow of doubt.

Key 16 depicts this awakening to the reality that we no longer need to remain in ignorance. As we awaken to reality, we live in darkness between lightning flashes. Finally, after hundreds or thousands or even hundreds of thousands of flashes, we enter the land of starlight. But while we linger here between the world of absolute darkness and starlight, we remain in ignorance most of the time. We live in a raging storm. We reside in uncertainty. We don't know if we'll survive or not.

We fear the darkness more because we've seen there can be light. We fear our ignorance. We become angry with ourselves, with the Universe. We express this anger in our life with our family and friends. We live in a fearful and angry world. This is the spiritual message of the Tower.

The rest of the message is to get out of here. Seek knowledge. Be done with ignorance. Follow the light and quit the darkness. That's the message of the Tower too. Grasp on to the next Star of Hope you see and move into the dim starlight away from almost complete darkness. That's what Key 16 and Universal Law Sixteen have to teach us.

17

Universal Law Seventeen says there's hope for all those who see the light, however dimly, and pursue it. This is the same thing as saying there's hope for the ignorant who believe in knowledge, for if they persist, knowledge will be theirs.

Key 17 depicts the starlight into which we move as we continue to combat our ignorance. This is the Star of Hope that can answer all our prayers. It's the Star of Navigation by which we can find our way out of the darkness. It's the Star of Meditation which is the path out of our ignorance. It's the Star of Bethlehem which promises us we can become a reborn and regenerated person. It's the Water Star which reminds us to remember who and what we truly are.

We've taken our second step to overcome our ignorance. We're beginning to understand a little bit about who and what we truly are. We're beginning to have a little faith in the Universe. We're beginning to believe there might be a Creator God, a Father/Mother God. We're beginning to believe we may just all be in this together. At least we have that much hope.

The Star promises if we meditate, if we go within ourselves, we'll discover the truth about ourselves. As we learn this truth, the moon rises and the light changes. We'll take that step next time.

18

As we move from complete darkness and abject ignorance (Key 15—the Devil) to cosmic consciousness and absolute enlightenment (Key 21—the World), we move step by step into greater and greater light. From absolute darkness (Universal Law 15) we moved on to occasional flashes of light (Universal Law 16). From there we moved into the dim starlight (Universal Law17). Our knowledge grew ever so slightly from complete and merciless ignorance (Devil) to occasional insights into our true reality (Tower). From there we began to see the reality of life but very dimly (Star).

As darkness and ignorance are the birthrights of most of humanity, so this world of delusion is the bane of sincere spiritual students. First there's ignorance. Then we see a little light, we become exposed to a reality deeper than ourselves. We begin to believe there might be more to life than we know. We step out into the storm and lightning occasionally lights our way. We grasp onto little pieces of knowledge and we begin to learn the truth about ourselves. We've moved from the grip of Universal Law Fifteen to Universal Law Sixteen.

Those of us who continue our spiritual journey eventually step out into the starlight. We begin to see things we never knew existed before. We can't make them out but we see they're there. We begin to understand there's more to life than working, eating, sleeping, and sex. But at this stage of our spiritual development, we don't have any answers. What we have are questions and a desire for answers.

Now we move into the moonlight, into a world where we see reality hidden in the darkness. We also see illusion in the darkness. We delude ourselves some of the time and we appear to understand ourselves the rest of the time. We've reached the domain of Key Eighteen. We're under the influence of Universal Law Eighteen.

Universal Law Eighteen tells us to stop fooling ourselves about who and what we truly are. When we encountered Universal Law Fifteen we thought we were our body, our job, our thoughts and ideas. Universal Law Sixteen taught us to awaken to our true reality and helped us attain a small glimpse of that reality. Universal Law Seventeen taught us to go inside ourselves to learn more about who and what we truly are.

Universal Law Eighteen promises us that we can attain complete knowledge about ourselves. We can learn who and what we truly are. We can find the lessons we need to learn and we can learn those lessons. We can know our life's purpose, our reason for being here on this earth at this time.

That's the promise of the Moon, Key 18. It's also a responsibility incumbent upon each and every one of us. We have a duty to every other human being to discover our life's purpose and fulfill that purpose. If we don't, nobody else will do it for us.

We came into this life for a purpose. We brought with us an arsenal of talents to overcome the obstacles we knew would probably face us. We have a responsibility to discover the purpose of our life, use our talents, and overcome the obstacles we suspected would be there.

19

When we realize the truth of these things, we move from the moonlight into the sunlight. We become regenerated human beings with the power and resolve to do the things we agreed to do to fulfill our life's purpose.

Universal Law Nineteen tells us we'll become regenerated when we realize our life's purpose. We leave behind our illusions and delusions. We see ourselves for what we truly are. We know our life's purpose. We know how to use our talents to overcome the obstacles in our life. We become regenerated. We have new energy to do the things we must do.

We understand our duty and we perform it. By moving into full sunlight we see everything as it is. We no longer have doubts; we know. Our darkness is shattered with full and complete light. Our ignorance is conquered with truth, and the truth indeed sets us free.

We're free to be who and what we really are. Free to perform our duty, to fulfill our destiny. Free to identify and use our talents for the benefit of all. Free to tackle and overcome every obstacle placed in our way. Free to be regenerated.

That's the message and the promise of the Sun, Key 19. We're basking in full sunlight. Could there be anything better?

20

Universal Law Twenty says we have the ability to advance spiritually to the point where we live in this world and the spiritual world at the same time.

When we attain the level of Universal Law Nineteen our spiritual light is as bright as the Sun which warms this world. We become reborn as new human beings. We become spiritual masters. We realize Deity is all there is. We rise above the mundane concerns of this world and accept all there is as our brother and sister.

What could be better than this? We've arrived, no? We're enlightened, no? We know who and what we really are—a son or daughter of God. Right? Right!

But Universal Law Twenty lets us know beyond any shadow of doubt, there's more to life than being reborn as a new and revitalized human being. We can become more spiritual. We can become unconditionally loving.

We reside in our Soul. Our Soul is thousand times brighter than our Sun. We become a beacon of light for all spiritual travelers. We become an adept. We live in a spiritual world but maintain a physical body for the purpose of teaching others they can attain what we've attained. We've become a saint on Earth, a great spiritual leader. We become a source of energy for others, a spiritual dynamo.

21

Universal Law Twenty-One teaches us we can become even more spiritual. We can walk this Earth in the spirit and be a spiritual guide to others. We can take physical form when necessary, or we can take astral form in our soul body, but we normally reside in our spiritual body. We guide others along the pathway of liberation we've traveled.

We've become an ascended master. We reside in our Spirit. Our Spirit shines a thousand times brighter than our Soul. We're beings of pure light. There's no darkness in us. We're filled with absolute knowledge. There's no ignorance in us. We've attained the goal of this life, the goal of many lifetimes.

While residing in complete darkness (Key 15) we gained knowledge about our true selves if we chose to lose the chains of bondage. We advanced to occasional flashes of insight (Key 16) and within ourselves we knew there was a truth greater than ourselves. By continuing to learn more about who and what we really were, we came to dim knowledge, we walked in the starlight (Key 17).

Only by continuing to serve others and learn more about our true nature we were able to advance into the moonlight (Key 18). We could see reality but it was hidden from us in the shadows of illusion which kept us so long in ignorance. We've come from complete darkness to partial illumination, from absolute ignorance about our true nature to only partial ignorance, and partial knowledge.

Many of us reside in these four worlds, the worlds of darkness to partial illumination. The worlds of ignorance to partial knowledge about who and what we really are. If we continue to learn more and more about our true nature by turning within, we're reborn (Key 19) into our true nature. We gain spiritual knowledge about our true nature.

We rise above the Wheel of Karma. We can leave this plane of existence and never return to this dual world of good and evil. This world of love and hatred.

A few adepts do choose to return as spiritual teachers. They can also choose to seek more knowledge about themselves and become a spiritual adept (Key 20) and eventually an ascended master (Key 21). As an ascended master they reside in three worlds (body, astral, and spiritual). These same three worlds have always been with us. We learned the truth about ourselves. We understood our true nature and we learned to reside in the astral and spiritual worlds as well as our material body.

We returned to full knowledge about ourselves.

22

The Twenty-Second Universal Law is also called Universal Law Zero and it corresponds to the Fool in the tarot deck. This Law is all-encompassing. In its most simple form the Twenty-Second Universal Law states that "God is All," or "Allah is All," or "Isis is All," or "Brahman is All," or "The Divine is All." Substitute the name you use for the one creator God or Goddess. Say that name and follow it with the words "is all."

Deity is everything. Deity is Fire, Air, Water, and Earth. Deity is the birds and the trees, the wind and the rivers, the lakes and the mountains, the oceans and the fish. Deity is life and death. Deity is Spirit. Deity is you and me. Deity is everything.

This is the great lesson we learn as we travel the Path of the Sun and the Path of Judgment and the Path of the World. This is the great lesson we begin to learn with little flashes of insight as we travel the Path of the Tower, the lesson we suspected while we traveled in darkness on the Path of the Devil.

This is the great voyage we take after we awaken all our seven minds and learn the seven great lessons of life. These lessons we learned in the first fourteen Universal Laws are exemplified by Keys 1 through 14. These lessons prepared us to release ourselves from ignorance and seek the truth. That is what we do on the final seven stages of our spiritual journey. These final seven stages lead us through the fFifteenth to the Twenty-First Universal Laws exemplified by Keys 15 through 21.

From the Creator we went forth and to the Creator we return.

We are the Fool. We are the Twenty-Second Universal Law. We are the Law of Zero. We are a son or daughter of the Divine. We are a part of the Divine. Each and every one of us is an individualized expression of the Divine. That's who and what we truly are.

We forget who and what we truly are and we live in darkness, in ignorance, until we suspect the truth. We move from darkness to light, from ignorance to partial truth, and from partial truth to absolute truth. Then we do it all over again.

We are the Fool. We go forth to learn and to experience, to find our true selves. Then we go home from whence we came. Over and over again we do this until we become the perfected One we were in the beginning. Then we go forth no more. We have become everything we could be. We've become what we were in the beginning—perfect in every way. That's the message of the Fool and the message of the Twenty-Second Universal Law.

CHAPTER 3

The Cabala

Part One—Awareness

The Book of Genesis begins with: "In the beginning, God created the heavens and the earth." Three things are mentioned in this first sentence: God, heavens, and earth. In this article, we'll call this first God mentioned in the Western theology as Creator God or simply as the Creator for the sake of clarity.

This creation story is told in every commonly known religion. The principal character in this story is called by many names (Ahura Mazda, Brahman, Ptah, and Yod Hey Vav Hey, for example). The other two characters are called male and female, heaven and earth, light and darkness, energy and form, and several other pairs of opposites.

This is the nature of the Tree of Life. One creates two who are opposite in nature and those two combine to form one balanced whole. This is where we'll start our discussions since this is where Gnostics started to become separated from the other Western religions and spiritual paths.

Gnosticism is not so much a religion as it is a spiritual path. It is this spiritual path which is disclosed by the Tree of Life. This is the topic of our discussion.

If Creator God created the heavens and earth we know Creator God must have existed prior to this creation. On this assumption alone man has tried to define Creator God for thousands of years. We're no closer to arriving at a perfect definition now than we were back then.

Our second assumption is Creator God created something Creator God knew and understood. We all create things we know and understand. We don't create things we don't know and we don't understand. So what Creator God created was familiar to Creator God.

If Creator God knows all about each of us, because Creator God did create us, then Creator God knows more than all of us put together. In fact, Creator God knows everything we know and knows more than we know. Thus, because Creator God knows everything, Creator God has to be Omniscient.

If Creator God was all there was in the beginning, then there was only one thing Creator God could have used to create and that one thing was Him, Her, It, Creator God. therefore everything that is created is within Creator God, and Creator God is within everything. Creator God is both Omnipresent and Immanent.

If Creator God created us and all that is within Creator God, then all the power that is must exist within Creator God. Creator God is and must be Omnipotent. Additionally, since Creator God created the heavens, and there is no end to the heavens, and those heavens are within Creator God, then Creator God must be Infinite.

If Creator God was in the beginning and Creator God is Infinite then it follows that Creator God is also Eternal and Ever-living. So, we know Creator God is Eternal, Infinite, Omnipresent, Immanent, Omnipotent, Omniscient and Creator God created all that exists. Everything is Creator God. Creator God is everything.

If we assume Creator God created something He, She or It knew and understood, then it follows that the Law of Correspondence may be true. That Law says "That which is above is as that which is below; and that which is below is as that which is above." In short, this law is "As above, so below."

This gives us the opportunity to understand more about Creator God because the Law of Correspondence says we create in the same manner. How do we create?

We create because we get the idea we can create, we think we can create so we set about creating. We might intuit this idea, reason it out for ourselves, or receive it from some Higher Source. This logic leads to several possible ways in which Creator God came to create all that exists.

One possibility is Creator God received the inspiration to create Heaven and Earth from a Higher Source. In this case, we drop our consideration of this particular "Creator God" and go back to the Original Source above and beyond which there is no other Higher Source. In other words, we disregard this possibility since we've already decided there is no Higher Source above the Creator God we're considering.

If Creator God reasoned it out or intuited the idea to create a physical universe, the first step in this process was to become aware such a creation was possible. As above, so below.

To understand this process let's examine the life of a child. The first thing a child does is cry. Why? The child has become aware of something and reacted to that something. This is the story of a child's life: to become aware of something and react to it. This is the story of life for most humans most of the time. As we go through life, we become aware of many things and possibilities. Once we become aware, we start to think and have feelings about the things in our awareness.

As below, so above. Before Creator God could create anything, Creator God first needed to become aware of the possibility of creating anything. Awareness is the first step of this or any other creation.

On the Tree of Life, the topmost sphere is called Kether (pronounced ket'—er) or The Crown. In the Tree of Life we're creating now, we'll call this sphere Awareness. For our purposes, Kether, the Crown, and Awareness are all the same thing. What we know about one, we know about the other.

The Qabalah teaches that Awareness is partially manifest and partially unmanifest. It is partially of the world of creation and partially of the world above and beyond the creation. Awareness is like that. It's both partially in our consciousness and partially in our conscious mind. We're aware, but we're only aware of what we see, hear, smell, touch, taste or feel (intuit).

The Creator created everything that ever was, is now, or ever will be. The first step in this creation process was the act of becoming aware it was possible to create. Awareness precedes everything else. It's the first step in thinking everything we think, feeling everything we feel, speaking everything we speak, and doing everything we do.

According to the teaching of the Qabala, nine more steps are needed to actually manifest anything in the material plane. But none of those steps will occur until and unless there is first Awareness of the possibility of creating something in our lives.

Awareness is the first step, the first of ten steps to manifestation. Awareness is the first sphere on the Tree of Life, the first of ten spheres of manifestation. Awareness is the first act of creation, it is the first creation from which all else flows.

According to the Big Bang Theory, in the beginning there was nothing. At a point in this nothingness all the matter and energy that ever was, exists now, and ever will be was created. All this energy and all this matter were compressed into a single point, a single point in the Mind of the Creator.

The sheer power of all this energy being compressed into a single point caused it to explode in a Big Bang. Matter and energy have been moving away from the explosion of this single point ever since. Matter and energy will continue to speed away from this explosive beginning until the energy of that explosion has been expended. Then, according to the Big Bang Theory, everything will reverse course and be pulled back to its source in the Mind of the Creator.

Nobody knows for sure when the Big Bang occurred nor when it will collapse back on itself. Scientists are looking back in time toward the center of the Universe with very powerful telescopes. They say the Big Bang occurred about twelve billion years ago and that our Sun is about five billion years old.

These same scientists say the Universe is still expanding and it's not slowing down. Not yet. The best minds working on the Big Bang Theory guess the Universe will continue to expand for at least another ten to fifteen billion years.

To think it all began because Creator God became aware creation was possible. As above, so below. To think that all we are, have been, and ever will be is so because you and I became aware we could create our own lives. This Awareness was the first step in our own act of creation.

The Creator has been called many things. In the tradition of the Universal Gnostic Church, the Creator is usually referred to as Creator God. In Eastern traditions the Creator is called Brahman. In Greek myth,

Gaia emerged from the Chaos and created the Earth and everything in it. Thus the Creator can be considered to be Chaos though some call Gaia the Mother of All.

Tellus Mater was the Roman Goddess equivalent to Gaia and she, too, was born of the Chaos. In our discussions, we'll consider Chaos to be the Creator in both Roman and Greek mythology. The Creator of the Mesopotamians was the God El, the father of all man and creator of all things. The Creator in Egyptian mythology was Atum the self-created, the Great He–She. Memphis priests taught that Atum was the child of Ptah but this was apparently not a widespread belief.

In Irish Druidism the Creator is a goddess called Danu. She is the Great Mother of All that is and ever was. The name of the Creator in Norse mythology is lost to us. Many consider the Creator to be Tiwaz but the stories seem to indicate Tiwaz was born of the Creator.

The North American Indians were not one faith or religion but many. The Creator has as many names as there are tribal families. The Pueblo Indians consider the Creator to be Awonawilona. Awonawilona is the One Who Contains Everything.

The Algonquin Nation called the Creator Kitchi Manitou and the name Manitou has been used by several tribes in describing the Creator. Certain of the Pacific Coast Nations called this same God by the name Olelbis. To the Pawnee Nation this God is Tirawa-Atius and to the Cherokee it's Kanati and Selu (father and mother) who created all that is.

You need to decide for yourself what name you'll use for the Creator who, according to the Western theology, created the Heavens and Earth. Which is to say, the Creator created all that is, was, and ever will be.

Part Two—Intention and Belief

"In the Beginning, God created the heavens and the earth" according to the Book of Genesis. Several creation stories start out in the same vein. The words are different, but the concept is the same. Some say God first created the light and the dark. Others say the first creation was male and female, masculine and feminine energies.

The Heavens are boundless, endless. They go on forever. Earth is bounded, finite. It's a definite thing and well-defined. The more we study the early creation stories, the more we become convinced the first creation was to create matter and energy.

According to Einstein's Theory of Relativity, matter and energy are two different expressions of the same thing. Matter and energy can each be converted into the other. More than that, everything in the whole known Universe is either matter or energy and the sum of all the matter and all the energy is the Universe.

This sounds like, "In the beginning was God, and God thought about matter and energy and God was matter and energy." All the matter and energy that ever was or ever will be is here now, and all that matter and energy is the Creator. The Creator is probably more than all the matter and energy, but all that matter and energy are the Creator.

There's nothing in this story to tell us which came first, matter or energy. Consequently, every religion has a theory based on the major culture of that religion. Christianity teaches man came first. So do all the major Western religions. Most Pagans believe the All-Mother, or Great Mother came first.

Gnostics are not in agreement about this either. Some are in the "Man-came-first" camp while others stand firm knowing "Woman-came-first." Science says they came together, one cannot exist without the other.

The Big Bang started out as a point of combined mass and energy and the energy of that primal explosion is still propelling that matter through space. Matter and energy work together. You can't have one without the other. They both live and act together within the Creator and they are the Creator.

Energy is a boundless force and it expands forever. This is the "Heaven" of the first creation. This is the masculine principle called "Force."

Matter is form. It restricts and confines energy. This is the "Earth" of the first creation. This is the feminine principle called "Form."

The Creator is both form and force, matter and energy, masculine and feminine. All the matter and energy, force and form are the Creator but the Creator is more than just that.

Most of the ancient writings about the creation allude to the male and female archetypes rather than explicitly naming them. For example, Genesis refers to this phase of creation as "God created the heavens and the earth." The Jerusalem Talmud explains this as a process of the one Creator God dividing Itself into two things of opposite polarity. Usually, this is explained as being the Void which is of negative polarity and the Substance. Some Christian theologians consider the Angelic World to be the Heavens and Manifestation to be the Earth.

Eastern philosophers look at creation in very much the same way. Brahman, the one Creator God, became the Male and the Female principle without diminishing Brahman. In this philosophy the One became Three in One. That's pretty close to the Western concept of the Trinity. The Two, male and female, cannot exist without the One, but the One is self-existent with or without the Two.

The other interesting thing about the Two is that one cannot exist without the other. The Male Archetype cannot exist without both the Creator Archetype and the Female Archetype. The Female Archetype cannot exist without both the Creator Archetype and the Male Archetype. The Creator Archetype can exist with or without the Male and Female Archetypes.

In many religions, the Great Mother gave birth to her husband and together they gave birth to all that exists. In others, the male came first as in the story of Adam and Eve. In the Qabalah, the Creator (which may be called the Great Mother or the Great Father) came first. The Creator separated Itself into two parts while retaining the whole of Itself. These two parts are the Mother of All Things and the Father of All Things. They are the Light and the Darkness, the Positive and the Negative, the Male and the Female Principles, the Male and Female Archetypes.

There really is no discussion about which came first, the man or the woman. The answer, according to the Qabalah, is they came together. One Archetype cannot exist without the other. They are opposites, and when they come together they are the Creator. But the mystery is that even if they don't come together, the Creator exists in Its, His, or Her fullness and is not diminished in any way.

The Great Mystery has a very simple explanation. If the Male and Female Archetypes exist in the Mind of the Creator, then it makes sense that the Creator is not diminished. If the Mind of the Creator is that which gets divided, then it makes sense that neither the Male nor Female Archetype can exist without the other. These Archetypes are opposites and to think of the attributes of one is to define the attributes of the other.

The Creator is the One Mind and creation is in the Mind of the Creator.

That's the great secret of all the Western and Eastern Mysteries. Everything is Mind. Everything is the Creator. Nothing exists outside the Mind of the Creator. Everything exists within the Mind of the Creator. We are all brothers and sisters in the creation of all that exists. We're all in this same Mind together. We're all interconnected not only to our friends but to our enemies. We're connected to all the plants, animals, and minerals in this world. Everything is the Creator.

The Creator is unconditional love, all knowing, all powerful, present everywhere, and in all things. This is the archetype that is the Creator. It's the root of the Air Element.

The Father archetype is outgoing energy that moves away from the source. It expands in all directions as it moves. This energy is a force that moves things. Because it moves, we call it positive. The Father archetype is all about intention, the desire to do something, the ability to conceive it, the resolve to do it, and the energy to finish what is started. It's the root of the Fire Element.

The Mother Archetype is ingoing and does not move. It is inert but collects energy inside itself. It's a form that contains things, and because of this we call it negative. The Mother Archetype is all about receptivity, the capacity to feel it, the inertia to contain it, the ability to remember it, and the ability to love it forever. Mother is the root of the Water Element.

On the Tree of Life, the Creator occupies the topmost sphere. All energy moving down through the Tree of Life originates in this topmost sphere. The Father Archetype occupies sphere number two on the right-hand side of the Tree of Life as you're looking at the Tree. The Mother Archetype occupies sphere number three on the left-hand side of the Tree of Life as you're looking at the Tree. These two spheres are located below the first sphere. All three are interconnected so as to form a triangle with the Creator Archetype at the top. The sphere for Father is called Intention (Chokmah) and the one for Mother is called Belief (Binah).

This triangle is called the Triangle of Air. It's also called the World of Air because everything in this world is thoughts and ideas. Nothing else exists in this world except thoughts and ideas. It's the Archetypal World or the World of Archetypes. It's also called the Spiritual Triangle among several dozen other names.

Some authors consider the Archetypal World to be a Trinity that includes God the Creator, Father God and Mother God. In Christian Gnosticism this trinity is often called Father–Mother–Creator God or Creator–Father–Mother God. It's also called Creator–Mother–Father God. The three spheres in this triad can therefore be labeled Creator God, Father God, and Mother God in that order. The Creator Archetype, Father Archetype, and Mother Archetype is another way of saying the same thing as is Creator–Male–Female Archetypes. Awareness, Intention, and Belief are the definitions of these three concepts.

Several authors assign different Judeo-Christian God names to these spheres. The most common assignment of Divine Names is Eheieh to Kether (Creator), Yah to Chokmah (Father) and Yod Hey Vav Hey Elohim to Binah (Mother). Eheieh is often translated as "I am That I am" or as "I am What I am." Yah is Father God, Yod Hey Vav Hey is the Tetragrammaton normally rendered as Jehovah or Yahweh, and Elohim is Father and Mother God. Some claim Elohim is a singular male God and plural female Goddesses.

Your assignment, should you decide to experiment with the World of Archetypes, is to assign one God or Goddess from the pantheon of your choice to each of the spheres in this trinity. It's important to preserve the sequence of Creator–Male–Female Archetypes for these first three spheres. But the name of the Deity assigned to each is entirely up to you.

Part Three — The Abyss

The Archetypal World, the World of Air is separated from the rest of the Tree of Life by an Abyss "of endless breadth, depth and width." It's so deep you can't see the bottom of the pit, you can't see anything as you look down except endless space. It's so wide it appears to go in either direction forever. The other side is so far away you can't see it. You're not even sure there is another side. Standing on the edge of this abyss, it feels like you're standing on the edge of the world looking out into nothingness. At least, that's what most of the mystics who've been there have to say.

Yet, when we look at the Tree of Life, we see paths connecting each of the three topmost spheres to each other. We also see five paths from these three crossing the Abyss; one from the Creator and two from both the Father and Mother Archetypes.

These five paths are called the Impassible Paths because crossing the Abyss is impossible until and unless you've completed all the requirements to do so. We'll discuss those requirements over the next couple of months, But in short, they can all be summed up in the admonition to love your Creator and your neighbor as yourself.

The Abyss not only separates the World of Air from the rest of the Tree of Life, it reflects the first three Sephira into the next level of the Tree. As a result of this reflection, the second triangle is upside down relative to the first. It is a reflection like a pool of water might reflect that which is above it. If the second triangle on the Tree is a reflection of the first, then the second triangle isn't real at all. It's just a reflection. Reflections aren't real.

Some of the modern theories about the birth of the universe would agree with this point of view. The modern concept accepted by most physicists is the universe is a hologram within the mind of some vast intelligence. It doesn't take much of a leap of faith to believe that Intelligence is the Creator as expressed through the Father and Mother Archetypes.

Science continues to prove the Gnostic viewpoint in all things.

The Sepher Yetzirah, which is the first written document we know as the Qabala, teaches that Spirit breathed (Air) and from this breath came the "The Great Waters." Air came first and Water second. The Sepher Yetzirah continues explaining that Water carried Fire in Her belly. Desire (Fire) comes from the belly and is a combination of Air and Water but desire (Fire) is born of Water. Desire is born from our emotions.

Here's a little exercise to help you understand the Abyss a little better: Stand in front of a mirror. Point both your index fingers like guns. Point these "guns" at the mirror and slowly move them forward until they touch the mirror. In this example, your shoulders are the Father and Mother Archetypes above the Abyss. The reflection of your shoulders is Daughter and Son on the other side of the Abyss. The mirror represents the Abyss. Both your arms and the reflection of your arms are the connecting path between these spheres. They connect at the mirror but each remains in its own world and does not encroach into the world of the other.

This is actually a fairly good analogy. The spheres above the Abyss are in a different world than those below. The spheres below are a reflection of the spheres above. The spheres above are connected to the spheres below through the Abyss. But since that which is above and that which is below the Abyss do not cross the Abyss, this connection is between two different kinds of things. The two kinds of things do not mix, they connect. They touch each other at the Abyss.

The only thing that crosses the Abyss is our consciousness. Our bodies never cross the Abyss nor does our personality. Our thoughts, ideas, memories, and attitudes cross the Abyss but our emotions and our desires do not. When we cross over the Abyss from above all we bring with us is our thoughts, ideas, and attitudes. We leave our memories behind in the World of Air, the World of Archetypes.

Part Four—Love, Power, and Harmony

Spanning the Abyss is a path running down the right-hand side of the Tree of Life from Father God to Daughter God directly below. Also spanning the Abyss is a path running down the left-hand side of the Tree of Life from Mother God to Son God or God the Son directly below.

Father God is the Father Archetype and the Male Archetype. Mother God is the Mother Archetype and the Female Archetype. Daughter God is the Daughter Archetype and the Maiden Archetype. Son God is the Son Archetype and the Knight or Young Man Archetype.

These archetypes each have many variations and definitions. An interesting exercise is to start a page in your journal for each of the five major archetypes we've already discussed. Then add other possible names and attributes for each over the course of several weeks or months.

For example, the Creator Archetype also includes such other archetypes as architect, artist, author, builder, designer, discoverer, founder, inventor, and producer. Any type of creative endeavor is a candidate for classification under the master symbol of the Creator. As we examine the Son and Daughter Archetypes we find two very interesting facts:

First, the only energy coming down the Tree of Life into Daughter comes from Father and the energy coming down into Son comes from Mother. The energy from above changes polarity as it crosses the Abyss. The Male gives birth to the Female and the Female gives birth to the Male.

Second, the only energy from the other "parent" comes through the first. Mother God sends energy across to Father God and that's the only female energy that goes down to Daughter God. Father God sends energy across to Mother God and that's the only male energy that goes down to Son God. It's difficult to understand how the polarity can change in such an arrangement.

Daughter God is the fourth Sephirah on the Tree of Life and its Hebrew name is Chesed (Hess' - ed) which means Mercy. Mercy is also called Charity, Love, and Unconditional Love. Mercy is the archetype of the loving daughter. But, remember Mercy is a reflection of the Father–Mother–Creator Archetype. So the Father–Mother–Creator Archetype contains the loving Daughter.

Son God is the fifth Sephirah on the Tree of Life and it's Hebrew name is Geburah which means Severity. Severity is also called Strength, Power, Trepidation, Chaos, and Conflict. Pachad is another Hebrew name assigned to Son God. Pachad means Fear or Trepidation. All of these names are assigned to this sphere and the Son of God, the Son of the Goddess or the Widow's Son. (That's a long story in itself because the Black Widow is Binah, the Mother Archetype. She's also the Black Madonna.) Power is the archetype of the God of War and the warrior and this warring son is contained within and is a reflection of the Father–Mother–Creator Archetype.

There's one more Child of Deity, but this child is a very special child. It receives energy from all of the first five Sephiroth. The Creator, Father, Mother, Daughter, and Son all send energy down into the sixth Sephirah. It is literally the child of all the Sephiroth above it. This Child of Deity is on the Middle Pillar directly below the Creator but on a level further down the Tree than both Daughter and Son. It completes the second triangle on the Tree of Life, the triangle reflected from above, the triangle reflected across the Abyss.

The name of this Sephirah is Tiphereth (Tiff' - er - et) which means Beauty. Other names assigned to Beauty include Harmony, Balance, Son of God, and Christ Consciousness or Krishna Center. It is the archetype for the Peacemaker, the Hanged God, and the Sacrificed or Crucified King. It's also a direct reflection of the Father–Mother–Creator Archetype.

The sphere attributed to the Daughter Archetype is called Mercy, Charity, and Love,. In the Order we usually refer to this sphere as Love, and by this we mean Unconditional Love.

The sphere attributed to the Son Archetype is called Severity, Strength, Fear, Trepidation, Anger, Sadness. and Power among other things. In the Order we usually refer to this sphere as Power and by this we mean to include the power of Anger, Fear, and Sadness.

The sphere attributed to Beauty or Harmony is also called Balance, Crucified, or Sacrificed God, the Crucified or Sacrificed Archetype, Service, the Grandchildren, the Grandchildren Archetype, and the Soul. In the Order we usually refer to this sphere as Harmony though we see the Creator as our Spirit and this center of Harmony as our Soul.

These three spheres form a downward-facing triangle which is a reflection of the upward-facing triangle of the World of Air. Each of the three spheres in this triangle are connected to each other. The Creator is directly connected only to our Soul (Harmony). Father is connected to both Daughter and Harmony. Mother is connected to both Son and Harmony. Everybody above is connected to the Grandchildren below.

This downward-facing triangle is a reflection of the upward-facing World of Air. It is the Child of Air. These three spheres in the lower triangle are reflections of the Archetypes. They are the reflection of thoughts and ideas.

Reflect on your own thoughts for a moment. You'll start to feel something. This something can be reduced to love, happiness, peace, and joy or it can be fear, anger, sadness, and indifference. The reflection of our own thoughts and ideas are the emotions of our life.

As above so below. As below so above. The reflection of the thoughts and ideas in the World of Air Above the Abyss are the emotions of the World Below, the World of Water, the World of Emotions.

The World of Air is separated from the World of Water by the Great Abyss. There is a great chasm between our thoughts and ideas and our emotions. There is a great chasm between thoughts and ideas and emotions in the Divine Mind.

In the World of Air, the male and female, Father and Mother Archetypes are the opposite of each other. You can't have one without the other. The Creator participates in both the male and female and is more than the sum of both.

In the World of Water this concept of opposites is carried one step further. Daughter is Mercy, Love, Charity, and Unconditional Love. Daughter is also the opposite of all these things. She's Indifference, Apathy, Intolerance, and Unkindness.

Son is Anger, Fear, Sadness, Severity, Strength and Power. He's also their opposites. He's Joyful, Peaceful, Happy, and Soft and his Strength and Power are used with Joy, Peace, and Happiness.

It's in that place called Harmony where all these positive and negative emotions come together, where they become balanced. Any expression of excessive positive or negative emotions is due to an imbalance in this area of our lives.

Here's the important secret taught by most mystery religions: Emotions are a product of our thoughts. We learn fear, anger, sadness, love, and all our other emotions. Our thoughts and attitudes control our emotions.

In our experience, the most difficult thing to accept about the Tree of Life is that our emotions are born in our thoughts and ideas, our attitudes, and belief systems. This concept blocked many of us from spiritual progress for several years. The skeptic in us couldn't accept anything about our minds having control of our emotions, p eriod. As far as we were concerned, our emotions were out of control, and thinking about them didn't make them any better.

But if you stop to think about it, it's all very logical.

We think. Because we think, we start to have feelings about our thoughts. Our feelings affect our thinking and it goes round in a circle. Our emotions feed our thoughts and our thoughts feed our emotions. We can work ourselves up into a dither in no time at all. We can also calm ourselves down and change our thinking.

If Unconditional Love is a decision, why do I instantly dislike certain people? It's all based on our memory of past experiences. Our memories store things based on the amount of emotion attached to those memories. The more emotional the memory, the easier it is to remember and we remember it more vividly. Since our memories are stored in our subconscious mind, we're not always aware we're reacting to something based on those memories.

The fact is we judge people based on our memories of that person, people who look, act, or behave like that person, people who speak like that person, or people who subconsciously remind us of that person. It doesn't matter who the person is, what matters is how we view that person based on our memory or past encounters with other people. We instantly dislike certain people because they remind us of one or more negative attributes of other people in our memory. We instantly like some people for the very same reasons.

Unconditional Love is a decision. We choose to love somebody or not. We choose to love something or not. We choose to love and we choose not to love. We choose to be indifferent toward certain people or things. We choose apathy over love. We choose the level of our commitment.

Anger is a decision. It may be conscious, subconscious, or even unconscious, but it is a decision. Conscious anger is often called "righteous anger." We're entitled to feel angry and so we do. Subconscious anger is a habit we've formed over time. We've been angry in this situation before and here we are again. Eventually, our anger can become so automatic it's done on an unconscious level. Our thoughts birth our anger.

Fear is a conscious, subconscious, or unconscious decision. We become anxious and our anxiety turns to fear. We worry about what could happen and our worry becomes anxiety, and our anxiety becomes our fears. If we expect the worst, we begin to worry that the worst will happen. If we expect the best, we begin to worry that the best will happen. Our thoughts birth our fears.

Sadness is a decision. It's a conscious, subconscious, or unconscious decision based on past memories collected by our senses of sight, hearing, touching, tasting, or smelling and the emotions we decided to connect to that memory.

We are the parent of our emotions. Our thoughts, ideas, attitudes, and beliefs give birth to our emotions. And we imbue our memories of people, places, things, and events with these emotions. We are the product of our entire lifetime of thinking, birthing, and growing our emotions. Study my emotions and you can understand my thinking, the thinking that gave birth to those emotions.

This is a very hard lesson to fully comprehend and understand. We talk to people who have hormonal imbalances that cause them great depression. Telling them they thought themselves into this depression is not a cure for their problem. Drugs are not a cure for their problem. The only cure is serious spiritual work and very few people are willing to invest the amount of time and energy to do spiritual work. It's a commitment and commitments take energy, time, and work.

Your assignment, should you choose to participate, is to ponder your emotions this week and see if you can trace them back to your own thoughts, ideas, and attitudes in your distant past.

Part Five—Paroketh

The Abyss separates the World of Air from the World of Water. It is the third veil on the Tree of Life. It is the third veil we must rend as we return to our Source from the World of Manifestation which is our physical universe. As we come down the Tree of Life we now reach the Second Veil. The Second Veil is called Paroketh which means Portal and it's the Portal through which we must travel to reach our Soul. It's also the Portal through which the first order member of the Golden Dawn must pass in order to become an Adept.

Paroketh is called the Veil of Illusion because what we see below this veil is an illusion. Reality is on the other side. Our soul resides in the true reality. Our ego and persona reside in the illusion of reality. Paroketh is also called the Curtain of Fire which refers to the fact that the World of Fire is located beneath the World of Water on the Tree of Life. As we descend into the matter we must cross this Curtain of Fire.

Additionally, Paroketh is called the Curtain of Water because as we ascend the Tree of Life from the World of Fire we're confronted by a Curtain of Water which we must part (like Moses and the Red Sea) to ascend further.

As we incarnate into this physical world, we move down the Tree of Life from our beginning in Awareness at the top of the Tree. We build our intentions and focus ourselves down to one primary purpose for incarnation in the World of Air—the first three spheres. In the teachings of the Order the body we inhabit here in the World of Air, the World of Archetypes is our Spirit. Our Spirit is our Higher Self, our own Holy Guardian Angel. It's our Spirit that decides to incarnate and decides upon our purpose for incarnation. It's our Spirit which our Unmanifest Self builds in the World of Archetypes as the first step in our physical incarnation.

Since we cannot move across the Abyss in our Spirit, the Order teaches that our Spirit creates our second body, our Soul. Our Soul lives in the World of Water, the Creative World where we create the essence of what we will become in the physical reality. Our Soul is in constant communication with our Spirit. Our Spirit knows everything our Soul knows and experiences, just as our Unmanifest Self above the Tree of Life knows everything our Spirit knows and experiences. And, since our Unmanifest Self is a "Spark of Light in the Consciousness of the Unmanifest Creator," the One Source of All-That-Is knows everything our Unmanifest Self knows.

Our Soul decides how we'll express Unconditional Love and all our other emotions in our lives so we can reach the goal of achieving our purpose in the physical reality. It's in the World of Water where the blueprint for our emotional reactions to life is created. It's here we plan the relationships of our life. It's in this world where we attune our emotions to our life's purpose. We build an Emotional Body and that Emotional Body is our Soul. In various paradigms, our Soul is also called our Etheric, Christ Body, Christ Consciousness, Conscience, Krishna Center, Krishna Consciousness, and our True Self.

The next step in our descent down the Tree of Life is to cross the Veil of Illusion, the Curtain of Fire. Just as our Spirit builds a body to exist in the World of Water, so our Soul builds a body to exist in the World of Fire. This body is called our Astral Body or our Ego Body and it is our Ego and our Astral essence. Our Ego is the complex building block upon which our physical body, persona, and personality are built. Our Ego resides in the World of Fire and it's in constant communication with our Soul.

It's important to realize not all Souls create an Ego and descend into the World of Fire. Not all Egos create a body and a persona and descend into the World of Matter, the World of Earth. Likewise, not all Spirits create a Soul and descend into the World of Water and not all Unmanifest Selves descend into the World of Air. Those who remain in the World of Fire we call Ghosts. Those in the World of Water we refer to as Astral Beings, Spirit Guides, or Animal Guides and we consider many to be Masters. Those who remain in the World of Air are Ascended Masters, Adepts, and Great Souls.

The fact that you and I inhabit a physical vehicle means we decided to manifest for some purpose and we entered the World of Archetypes, World of Emotion, World of Desire, and the World of Matter in that order. Our job is now to discover our original purpose and then accomplish those goals. That process is called "climbing or ascending the Tree of Life." It's also called evolution, alchemy path-working, and magick. This is just the opposite of our descent into matter which is called involution.

Part Six—Desire, Mind, and the Matrix

Once we descend through the Veil of Illusion, also known as Paroketh, we enter the World of Fire, the Astral World. In this world we build the foundation for our physical body. In this world the Universe builds the foundation for the suns and planets of the universe. This is the Astral World which is the foundation for the physical.

According to the Order of Spiritual Alchemy and the Magickal Order of the Golden Dawn, this is the World of Ego. It's the world of our ego. The first sphere in this world and the seventh sphere on the Tree of Life is called Desire. Its Hebrew name is Netzach which is usually translated as Victory. A better translation is probably "Firmness," meaning the firmness of our intentions and dreams. Hence, the name of "Desire." Other names like Passion, Drive, Devotion, Intention, and Ambition are also appropriate names as is Intuition. Our Desire center is the root of our intuition.

Desire is the manifestation of Fire in the Astral World. Desire is based in our original intentions before we started the final stage leading to our incarnation (incarceration) here on Earth. It's the closest thing we have in the Astral World to our Soul which resides in the World of Water. It's our spiritual center in the Astral World.

In our opinion, the Element of Fire is the most difficult of the four Elements to interpret in the Tarot. Astrologically we understand the drive, passion, desire and energy of Fire fairly well. But in the Tarot we attribute it to things like a person's career, their intuition, or their spirit.

Our Passion is more than just our career, it's all of our consuming interests and all of the energy we have in our life. Yes, Fire is intuitive. Yes, Fire is closer to Spirit than the other three Elements but it's really not the Element of Spirit in my opinion.

Our Fire is a place we can go in meditation to learn about our life's purpose, our mission in this lifetime. When we made the decision to incarnate, we determined what we really wanted to accomplish in this lifetime. That's our purpose, our reason for incarnating. We can find that reason in the World of Fire.

We've descended the Tree of Life from the World of Air, through the World of Water, through the Second Veil, and now find ourselves in the World of Fire. We've passed from the World of Reality into the World of Illusion. We've received our "Baptism by Fire" as we crossed through the Curtain of Fire. This is our third baptism by the way. We received a Baptism by Air into the World of Air when we became manifest in our Spirit. We received a Baptism by Water into the World of Water when we descended into our Soul. Now we receive a Baptism by Fire as we descend into our Ego.

Our Ego is clothed in the World of Fire by the Elements of Fire, Air, and Water. Fire is sphere seven, which we discussed last week and in the question above. Water is the ninth sphere to be discussed next. Air is assigned to sphere eight, which in Hebrew is called Hod, and that's our subject here. Before we get there though, it's interesting to note that our Spirit, Soul, and Ego are each composed of denser and denser Air, Fire, and Water as we descend from the Unmanifest down the Tree of Life to physical manifestation.

Sphere eight is the Air Element expressed in the World of Fire. It's our thoughts, ideas, and attitudes filtered through our emotions. These are neither the Archetypes we find in the World of Air (sphere one) nor the intentionally balanced emotions we find in the World of Water (sphere six). These are the raw, vibrant, energy-filled thoughts we have in our everyday mind. That's why we call sphere eight Intellect or Mind and it refers to our day-to-day intelligence.

Our Mind operates on three distinct levels: (1) Memory (Past), (2) Cognition (Present), and (3) Imagination (Future). Our complete memory contains both our subconscious and unconscious minds. Our subconscious mind is where we store memories we can normally access. Our unconscious mind stores all other memories. Our Cognitive Mind is our rational mind also known as our thinking mind. This is our logical and deductive mind with which we think and deduce. Our Imagination is our Imaginative Mind and this is where we plan our future and imagine the possibilities for our life.

Our Intellect is connected to our Emotional World in both Harmony and Power. This gives us the ability to draw upon our Inner Strength and our Inner Harmony (also called our Soul). Our Intellect is also connected to our Desire Center and this gives us some direction in focusing our thoughts. What we desire colors what we think. Lest you haven't figured it out already, both our Desire and Intellect are masculine qualities.

The first two worlds, the side spheres, which lie on the right and left pillars of the Tree, were balanced in that one was feminine and one was masculine. Now, in this second reflection of the Divine, we see an imbalance right-to-left. This imbalance will become important as we complete our study of the Tree of Life. For now, it's fun to think about these things.

The Tree of Life is a three-phase descent from the Unmanifest through the Three Worlds of Air, Fire, and Water resulting in

Manifestation in the World of Earth. The first world is the World of Air. It's composed of the three Elements: Air in sphere one, Fire in sphere two, and Water in sphere three. These are the Creator, Masculine, and Female Archetypes. The Creator is the center of balance between the Masculine and Feminine.

The second world is the World of Water. It's composed of the same three elements. Sphere four is Water, sphere five is Fire, and sphere six is Air. Remember, the Abyss separates the Second World from the First World and that the Second World is a reflection of the First. Notice also that the masculine has moved from the right side of the Tree of Life to the left as you move down from the World of Air to the World of Water as you face the Tree. The feminine moves from the left side of the Tree to the right as you move down the Tree from the First World to the Second.

The third world is the World of Fire. It's also composed of the same three elements of Fire in sphere seven, Air in sphere eight, and Water in sphere nine. All of this leads to the fact that sphere seven is the Element of Fire in the World of Fire. Our intentions and beliefs in the World of Air have been energized with emotional power in the World of Water. The result is our intentions have become emotionally charged when we reach sphere seven. Emotionally charged intentions are our passion, drive, and desires.

Harmony, Desire, and Intellect all send energy to the third sphere in the third triangle, in the Third World of the Tree of Life. This third sphere is the ninth sphere on the Tree of Life. Its Hebrew name is Yesod and this means "Foundation." This is the foundation of the physical universe.

Physical matter is built upon a Matrix of Energy. Physical matter is itself spinning energy. Modern physics has proven what Einstein postulated half a century ago, that energy = mass times the speed of light squared. Matter is energy. Our ancient brothers and sisters who understood the Qabalah centuries and millennia ago knew this. Modern science has only proven this fact in the last twenty-five years.

The Matrix of Energy upon which the physical universe is built is the Element Water. This element flows into all the forms that exist on Earth. So there you have it. In the World of Fire we have the same three elements of Air, Water, and Fire that we've seen in the World of Water and the World of Air. The masculine and the feminine have switched polarities as we move down the Tree of Life from world to world. In the last world, the World of Fire, the feminine has moved from the Left Pillar to the Middle Pillar. Balance is maintained by the third sphere representing the third element in each world. Thus in the World of Fire, Water is the balancing point.

As our consciousness crosses the Abyss, we experience a change in polarity and the right side of our body changes from feminine to masculine as we cross the Abyss. When our consciousness passes through the Veil of Illusion we experience another change in polarity. This time, however, our polarity is scrambled. Feminine Water changes to Masculine Fire, but Masculine Fire changes to Neutral Air and Neutral Air becomes Feminine Water. Thus it is in the World of Illusion, the Astral World.

Part Seven—Manifestation, the Four Worlds, & Three Pillars

The final sphere on the Tree of life is called Malkut or Malkuth in Hebrew. This is translated as "Kingdom" or "Manifestation." The three spheres in the World of Fire, Desire, Intellect, and Foundation, all send energy to Manifestation.

Manifestation receives energy from the higher spheres only through the three spheres in the World of Fire. Thus it is completely isolated from the higher worlds.

Manifestation is the Earth Element and it stands alone as the only sphere in the World of Earth. It receives energy directly from the Elements of Air (Intellect), Fire (Desire), and Water (Foundation). Harmony, which represents the Element of Spirit in the physical world, sends energy to Manifestation through the other three Elements.

The World of Air which is also the World of Archetypes is composed of Awareness (1 = Air), Intention (2 = Fire), and Focus (3 = Water). The World of Air is the home for our Spirit. Just as the World of Air is the first creation of the Unmanifest Creator, so is our Spirit our first body and it resides in the World of Air. Our Spirit resides in the World of Archetypes, thoughts, and ideas. Our Spirit is our original Archetype and the ultimate source of all our thoughts and ideas.

The World of Water, which is the Reflection of the First World, is composed of Love (4 = Water), Power (5 = Fire), and Harmony (6 = Air). Notice two things. One, the Elements of Fire and Water have switched places as we move from the World of Air to the World of Water. Two, the Element of Air remains in the middle. The World of Water is the home for our Soul. Just as the World of Water is a reflection of the World of Air across the Abyss, so is our Soul a reflection of our Spirit reflected across the Abyss. Our Spirit resides above the Abyss and does not cross over it to our Soul. Our Soul resides below the Abyss and does not cross over the Abyss.

The World of Fire, the second reflection of the First World over the Abyss and through the Veil of Fire, is composed of Desire (7 = Fire), Intellect (8 = Air), and Foundation (9 = Water). The World of Fire is the home of our Ego which is the reflection of our Soul. Just as our Soul doesn't cross the Abyss, our Ego doesn't cross the Veil of Water. Remember, the Veil of Ignorance seen from above is the Veil of Fire and seen from below is the Veil of Water. The Veil of Ignorance separates the Worlds of Water and Fire just as the Abyss separates the Worlds of Water and Air.

The World of Earth, the third and final reflection of the First World, is composed of only the tenth sphere Manifestation (10 = Earth) and is the sole representative of that Element. Our body resides in the World of Earth and within it is our three Elemental Bodies: Astral (Foundation = Water), Mental (Intellect = Air), and Intuitive (Desire = Fire). It also contains our Etheric, the energy field created by our physical body. Our body is home to our Ego, Soul, and Spirit. It's also home to our higher subtle bodies, which various traditions name in various ways. Let it suffice that we have one subtle body for each sphere from six on up to number one.

Notice that as we move down into the World of Fire, the Element of Fire switches from the left side to the right side of the Tree. This switching back and forth is the result of a change in polarity as we cross the Abyss and again as we cross the Veil of Paroketh. Thus the Right Pillar (as we're looking at the Tree) has Fire (Intention = 2) at the top, Water (Love = 4) in the middle, and Fire (Desire = 7) at the bottom.

The Right Pillar has several names. Among them are the Pillar of Fire, Pillar of Wisdom, Pillar of Knowledge, Pillar of Intention, Pillar of Desire, Pillar of Light, Jachin (which some call Joachim), the White Pillar, and the Left-hand of God. The Left Hand of God alludes to the fact that we turn around and step backward into the Tree of Life. The Right Pillar is the left side of our body.

Taken to another level, our left brain is associated with Intention; our left shoulder, arm, and hand are associated with Love = Compassion; and our left hip and thigh with Desire. The left side of our body is the Right Pillar.

The Left Pillar has Water (Belief) at the top, Fire (Power) in the middle, and Air (Mind or Intellect) at the bottom. Notice that Air is at the bottom of the Tree instead of Water as would be expected. This is one indication we have that the second reflection of the Archetypal World is more corrupt than the first reflection.

The Left Pillar has several names. Among them are Pillar of Water, Pillar of Cloud, Pillar of Understanding, Pillar of Faith, Pillar of Power, Pillar of Darkness, Pillar of Fear and Anger, Pillar of Anxiety, Boaz, the Black Pillar, and the Right Hand of God. The Pillar of Cloud is the pillar the Jews followed during the day on their forty-year journey through the desert on their way to the promised land. During the evening they followed the Pillar of Fire.

Taken to another level, our right brain, right shoulder and arm, and right hip and thigh are the Left Pillar of our body and they're associated with Belief, Power, and Mind in that order. In the Jewish Kabbalah the Left Pillar is the Right Hand of God, the Hand of Power.

Between these two pillars is the Middle Pillar which includes the spheres of Awareness, Harmony, Foundation, and Manifestation. Some Qabalists hold the middle pillar also includes the sphere that is not a sphere, the Sephirah that is not a Sephirah, the hole in the middle of the Abyss. This sphere that is not a sphere is called by many names. Among them is the Hebrew word Da'ath which means Knowledge or Learning. Other names for this Sphere are Emptiness, the Void, Enlightenment, and Consciousness.

The Middle Pillar has many names but it is most commonly referred to as the Middle Pillar. Other names include the Pillar of Harmony, the Pillar of Balance, the Pillar of Awareness, the Pillar of Consciousness, and the Pillar of Equilibrium. The Middle Pillar by any name becomes more important as you advance.

CHAPTER 4

The Tree of Life

Preliminary Notes

Almost every religion in the world teaches that "In the beginning the Divine created the world and everything in it"—or something to that effect. This universal belief that God or the Divine created everything is the basis for most if not all religions in the world.

What religions rarely agree upon is how the Divine created everything. Some claim this creation occurred instantly. Some claim it happened in six days about 5,000 years ago. Some claim the creation started about 120 billion years ago and is continuing to this day. Others claim the truth lies between these extremes. The Law of One does not address this issue. What you personally believe is a matter of personal belief. The Tree of Life does not address this issue either.

The Tree of Life is mentioned in the writings of the Sumerians thought to be nearly 6,500 years old. Through the centuries the Akkadians, Babylonians, Christians, Egyptians, Jews, Muslims, and Pagans have borrowed parts or all of these writings, added to them, modified them and incorporated them into their religious teachings. Yet the basic teachings remain the same.

The Creation

Most mystics agree that at some point in the ancient past, the Divine became aware it existed. Once this awareness happened everything became possible. Until this awareness occurred, nothing was possible.

There is great truth in these words because once we become aware of something, everything is possible in our own lives; but until we become aware of anything, nothing is possible. The lack of awareness makes us oblivious to our own opportunities. Only by becoming aware are we able to consider the possibilities of anything.

When we study consciousness, we learn there are three distinct attributes of consciousness. The most primitive and most limited is the concept of I. This is self-awareness. It is also the conscious mind. Most mystics believe the first step in the development of all consciousness is self-consciousness. Ancient peoples called this "I am" which means I exist or I am alive. When we apply this concept to the Divine, we call this awareness of the self I AM. I AM is a state of being something, a state of being. I AM is self-consciousness.

How long did the Divine exist before it became aware that it existed? How long has anything existed before you became aware of its existence? How long were you oblivious before you became aware? Think about these things and become more aware of yourself.

As consciousness grows it appears the next step is the awareness that not only am I alive, I am something. We are a being. More than that, we are a being that remembers our previous thinking and imagines future possibilities. These are stored in the subconscious mind where we can recall them at will. This is the consciousness called "I am that" by the ancients. When applied to the Divine we call this subconscious part of being I AM THAT. I AM THAT is sometimes referred to as Soul Consciousness or Higher Self Consciousness.

What are you? By meditating on this simple question you are probably mimicking the thinking of the Divine eons ago. We can all learn more about ourselves by using the Divine as our mentor and guide. Think about it. What are you?

Consciousness grows and eventually we become aware some of our memories are stored in the deepest levels of our being. Some things about us seem to be under the control of an "inner us" and happen without any apparent knowledge on our path in the deepest levels of our being.

That deepest level is our unconscious mind which remembers everything concerning us. In our unconscious mind we realize we are everything we ever were. We realize we are much more than we ever thought we were. When applied to the Divine we call this understanding at the deepest level of our being I AM WHAT I AM or I AM THAT I AM.

According to experts in early Hebrew, what the earliest words written about this facit of the Divine actually mean is I AM EVERYTHING. This really makes more sense if you consider the possibility that the Divine is Everything and everything is a part of the Divine. Unconscious memory is the memory of everything. The Divine remembers everything. Our own unconscious mind remembers everything about us. The Divine Unconscious Mind remembers everything about everyone and everything.

Since all of the creation exists within the Divine, the unconscious mind of the Divine knows everything about everybody and everything. This is what we call omniscience. The Divine is omniscient. This is the first essence of the Divine.

Since the Divine is everything, the Divine is also omnipresent. The Divine is a part of everything and everything is a part of the Divine. There is nothing that is not a part of the Divine. The Divine is everywhere. The Divine is omnipresent. This is the second essence of the Divine.

Finally, the Divine is omnipotent because all the strength of everything in the creation is the strength of the Divine. This is the third essence of the Divine. There is no power in the entire creation greater than the power of the Divine.

First, the Divine is omniscient, I AM.

Second, the Divine is omnipresent, I AM THAT.

Third, the Divine is omnipotent. I AM EVERYTHING.

And each of us is a child of that Divine.

This model of consciousness states that first there was self-consciousness and this is usually represented by a dot. Then there was subconsciousness which is represented by a line that makes a circle. Finally, there was unconsciousness which is represented by a circle with a dot in the middle. It is said that all consciousness is the circle whose center is everywhere and whose circumference is infinite. Inside this circle are an infinite number of dots. Each dot is a Tree of Life and that makes each of us a Tree of Life.

Each living and nonliving cell within our body is a dot. And each of those dots is a Tree of Life. Everything is a Tree of Life. Everything in the creation is a dot within an infinite circle; and that makes everything a living Tree of Life.

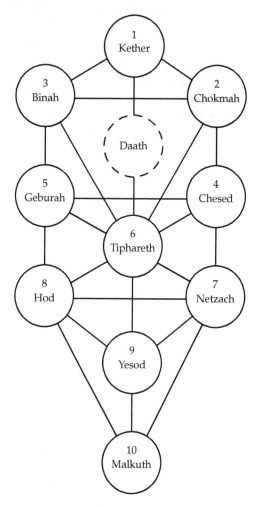

The Tree of Life

The Tree of Life, as shown above, is a glyph of the process of creation. It all starts with the White Sphere, the Sphere of Awareness. There are nine other spheres that cause the energy from the Sphere of Awareness to Manifest in this physical reality. They manifest the physical reality in this order: Gray, Black, Blue, Red, Yellow, Green, Orange, Purple, and the tertiary colors at the bottom of the Tree.

In each lesson, you will learn how to use that part of the Tree of Life to help you heal yourself on every level of your being. You will also learn how to create the life you want for yourself and how to become the truly spiritual person you came into this reality to become. There is no hocus-pocus. The only magick is you. The only alchemy is you. The Tree of Life is all about you becoming the spiritual being that you came here to become and doing the things you can here to accomplish.

In these lessons we use the word "Divine" to express a name for the Source of everything. You may substitute any name for the Divine that makes you more comfortable. You may use multiple names or a pantheon of names and the Tree of Life will explain to you exactly how you can heal yourself, how you can become the person you came here to become, and how you can accomplish the things you came here to do.

Lesson 1: The White Sphere

The white sphere at the top of the Tree of Life is that place within ourselves where we become aware we are alive, a being, we think and where we become aware of everything. This is the Sphere of Awareness, the Path of Being Aware or Being Oblivious.

We must be aware of incarnating into the physical reality before we can think about becoming part of this reality. Awareness is the first requirement. We must be aware that we can create, experience, or become something before we can even think about doing so. If we are not aware that we can do these things, we will never even consider doing them.

The Path of Awareness

The top sphere of the middle pillar, the white sphere at the top of the center of the Tree, has many names. Here is a list of a few of them with a short explanation:

- Crown—The "crowning glory" or the Radix of Glory called Kether, Ketter, or Kesser in Hebrew. God's crowning glory is seen as the creation of everything that exists.

- Union—The place where we unite with the Divine. It is also the place where we are created as a distinct living and conscious individual within the Mind of God. Though were are never ever separated from the Divine, we think we are.
- Divine Creator—The Divine becoming manifest is the creation according to these ancient teachings. This is because in the beginning there was nothing but the Divine. Hence, the Divine could create anything only by using itself.
- Primordial Point—This is a circle of infinite diameter with a central point everywhere. We call this omnipresence. This concept is also explained as Unity or the Vast Countenance—other names for the relationship between the Divine and that which is created.
- Lux Occulta—Hidden Light is another name for the Divine. While we are in the flesh we cannot see the Light that is the Divine. It is hidden from us. Thus it is called the Hidden Intelligence. This is also the Lux Interna, the Light Within which is both within us and hidden from us. For these reasons the Divine becoming manifest is also called the Existence of Existences and the Concealed of the Concealed.
- Ancient of Ancients—The Divine has already existed an infinite time and it is older than anything created by the Divine. The Ancient of Ancients has many similar names like the Ancient of Days.
- The Head which is not—This alludes to ancient wisdom only now being proven by quantum physics. That shocking revelation is that everything in the creation fluctuates between being here and not here. The consensus is we are manifest in the physical reality about half the time. That means we are not in this physical reality half of the time either. We flash in and out of this reality thousands upon thousands of times every second. Everything does. What we don't know is where we go the other half of our time.

The Function of the Path of Awareness

The function of this top sphere is to become aware. In the beginning of the creation, the Divine became aware it could create. Lacking this awareness the Divine could not even consider creating all the Divine has created. Awareness is the first step in learning, becoming, or creating anything. Without awareness nothing happens.

To begin doing anything, we must become aware that we can do it. Until we become aware, we may have the potential to do something, but we cannot do it since we lack the awareness that we can. Until we become aware we are completely oblivious of the possibility. When we become aware we have the ability to consider the possibilities. Until then we are oblivious.

Until you became aware you could crawl, you did not crawl. Until you became aware you could speak, you did not speak. Until you became aware you could walk, you did not walk. Until you became aware you could do something, you could not do it. You did not do it. In the beginning, you became aware through trial and error. But you did become aware and your awareness made it possible for you to learn how to do it.

We become aware on three levels of consciousness. Our mind operates on three levels of consciousness. The first level is the unconscious level. On this level of consciousness, we are completely aware of everything within and without ourselves. We are aware of everything in our environment.

The second level of awareness is on the subconscious level. Not much escapes our subconscious mind. But on this level of consciousness we are less aware than in our unconscious mind. We are oblivious to some things our unconscious mind is aware of.

The third level of awareness is on the conscious level. Here on this level, we are oblivious to many things that come into our sphere of awareness. In many ways we are more oblivious than aware. The more important something is to us the more aware we are about that thing. We are aware of everything in and around us on some level of our being. But more often than not we are not consciously aware of everything. Our subconscious mind may be and our unconscious mind is always aware of everything in and around us.

The Law of Awareness

The Law of Awareness indicates that when you become aware you can do anything you want to do. The corollary is that if you lack this awareness it will never dawn on you that you can do it. The Law of Awareness is that you can only do what you are aware you can do.

If you are not aware you can do it, you cannot do it. If you are not aware of the possibilities, you will never consider those possibilities. There are degrees of awareness and because you are partially aware, you have the opportunity to do some things imperfectly. If you ever become absolutely aware, you may have the ability to do some things perfectly. The more aware you are, the better you can function on every level of your being.

Lesson 2: The Gray Sphere

The gray sphere, the second sphere on the Tree of Life, is called the Path of Intention.

Some of the information we gain in the Sphere of Awareness, Sphere One at the top of the Tree of Life, grabs our attention and moves on into our Sphere of Intention. We may intentionally move it there. It may be a subconscious or unconscious process. Or it may just happen by chance. We don't really know why some things move into the Sphere of our Intentions.

The Path of Intention

The top sphere on the right-hand pillar of the Tree of Life as we look at the Tree is the Gray Sphere, the Sphere of Intention. This sphere has many other names, including:

- Ab or Abba—This means the same thing, "Father or Old Man". Older men were perceived in older times as wise elders. Ab and Abba both allude to the name the Supernal Father, meaning the Father above all other Fathers.
- Path of Wisdom—The Hebrew name for wisdom is Chokmah. In ancient times a man who survived to an old age was considered to be a wise person.
- Second Glory—The First Glory is the first sphere, the sphere of the Divine becoming manifest. The Second Glory is the second sphere from which we can see the face of the Divine becoming manifest. The hidden message is that our intentions allow us to see our awareness face to face. What we intend to do or become is a direct result of our awareness.
- Illuminating Intelligence—This alludes to the fact our intentions illuminate or shed light on our awareness; and our awareness sheds light on our potential intentions.
- The Formless One—Our intentions are the driving forces of our lives. Our intentions give us direction and purpose but they do

not give us form all by themselves. Intentions are formless. They are thoughts that may or may not mature into anything. Indeed, the vast majority of our intentions never mature into anything. They die on the vine.

• The Father of Sperm—Intentions are like sperm. There are thousands of sperm for every sperm that reaches its target. It alone matures into something. The rest die and are no more. The same is true of our intentions.

The Function of the Path of Intention

What we do know is that Sphere Two is where we create very simple to very complex intentions to do something. First we became aware of some information and dedicated our attention to it and now we form vague to concrete intentions to do something about this information. Or it just happens by chance.

Just as in our Sphere of Awareness, we become aware of much more information than we pay attention to or care about, so in our Sphere of Intentions we can form many more intentions in a day than we can accomplish in a lifetime. Intentions multiply. One intention leads to another and another. A few of these will actually become manifest in our lives.

Our intentions manifest on three levels: our unconscious mind, subconscious mind, and conscious mind. This means we are not always consciously aware of our intentions. The only way we can learn some of them is to study our actions. We cannot perform anything unless we have an intention to do so. Therefore, what we do is based on an intention of ours at some level of our being.

By studying our actions we can learn what intentions our subconscious and unconscious minds have that are affecting our actions. This gives us the opportunity to learn what our unconscious and subconscious minds are thinking.

The Law of Intention

The Law of Intention states that you can only do what you intend to do. If you intend to do it, you can do it. If you do not intend to do it, you cannot do it. We are all incapable of acting unless we first create an intention to act. Having created an intention to act does not mean that we will actually do that.

Lesson 3: The Black Sphere

The black sphere is Sphere Three on the Tree. It is called the Sphere of Belief. It is also the Sphere of Belief Systems. Our beliefs and belief systems are quite the opposite of our intentions because they restrict and limit what we can do with our lives. We select what intentions and information we can act upon based on our beliefs and belief systems. These things are the only things we can manifest in our lives.

The Path of Belief

Like the first two spheres, the Sphere of Belief has several other names:

- Mara or Marah, Mare and Mari—These three words all mean the Great Sea. But the Great Sea is the Subconscious World, the memory of ourselves.
- Ama and Aima—Ama is the dark sterile mother and Aima is the bright fertile mother. This refers to the feminine or receptive nature of Beliefs as opposed to the masculine outgoing nature of Intentions. Ama is the Mother of Disbelief and Aima is the Mother of Belief. Ama and Aima both allude to the Supernal Mother, the Mother above all other mothers.
- Binah—The Hebrew name for this sphere, Binah, is most often translated as Understanding. The Sphere of Understanding is where we understand our nature and our nature is to express ourselves based on our beliefs and our disbelieving.
- Sanctifying Intelligence—The Sanctifying Intelligence is based on faith because faith emanates from this place. Faith is based upon and expresses our beliefs.
- Parent of Faith—It is also called the Mother of Faith because Faith is the child of Belief. Our faith is an expression of what we believe and don't believe.
- Mother of All Form and Substance—The ancient teaching of the Kaballah is that the feminine gives form and substance to all things. Lacking belief nothing can take form or have substance.

The Function of the Path of Belief

Awareness (Sphere One) is neutral. It is neither masculine nor feminine but it contains both. Intention (Sphere Two) is masculine in nature.

Intentions expand in both scope and number. Beliefs are equal and opposite to intentions. Beliefs do not expand. They contract. They do not multiply. They resist expansion and they restrict what we think about every facet of our lives. This is the feminine attribute, to contain and nourish.

Belief systems are the framework that contain our beliefs. As the feminine contains the growing egg so do belief systems contain our growing beliefs. This is the exact opposite of the masculine. The masculine shoots out millions of sperm for every egg. Masculine intentions multiply and go forth; and most of them die without manifesting.

The Sphere of Belief is the mother of all things because until and unless we believe we can create something in ourselves or in our lives, we cannot. Henry Ford told his engineers that if they believed they could, or if they believed they could not, they were right. His message was that you cannot do what you believe you cannot do. His message was also that if you believed you could, you could.

Just because you believe you can't, you can't. Just because you believe you can doesn't mean you will. But it does mean you have the ability to do anything you believe you can do. You must first have the awareness that you can and the intention to do it. And if you believe you can, then all you have to do is do it.

The ancient teaching concerning this sphere is that it is the root of all things in the physical reality. It is the root of all energy and matter. This means all energy and matter are created because we consciously, subconsciously, or unconsciously believe we can do that.

As we continue our study of the Tree of Life we more and more understand that it is also the Tree of Invention and the Tree of Creation. The more we form our own intentions and beliefs, the further we move away from our childhood, our personal Garden of Eden where all was provided for us. We move into the World of Pain and Suffering where we intend and believe we can make a difference.

Lacking this awareness, intention, and belief we cannot create our own lives and accomplish the things we came into the physical to do. Once we have this awareness, intention and belief we can create miracles in our lifetime. Once we have this awareness, intention, and belief we really can do anything. The only issue then is whether we will selfishly do it for ourselves or spiritually do it for the benefit of all.

The Law of Belief

The Law of Belief states that you can create in your life and in yourself only what you consciously, subconsciously, and unconsciously believe you can create.

Another way of saying this is that you can create only to the extent that you believe in your ego, soul, and spirit that you can create. What you create and what you do not create is a direct result of your awareness, intentions, and beliefs. These things are modified by your attentive mind, remembering mind, and imaginative mind.

Lesson 4: The Blue Sphere

The blue sphere is our Path of Compassion. We decide how much or how little compassion and cruelty we will extend to everything in our sphere of awareness based on how we think about the information we have at our disposal. That information is the thoughts, ideas, words, pictures, and attitudes we created for ourselves in our World or Air.

This is the information we use to decide to be compassionate, merciful, loving, kind, and nurturing or ruthless, merciless, hateful, unkind, and cruel. This is the information we use to decide to be depressed, sorrowful, sad, happy, joyous, or ecstatic.

The Path of Compassion

The Sphere of Compassion has several other names, including:

- Mercy—The Hebrew word for mercy is Chesed. The ancient Hebrew concept of mercy was justice applied with unconditional love as much as was humanly possible under the circumstances. Their concept of vindictiveness was justice applied with malice and loathing.
- Love—This includes caring or not-caring, nurturing or retaliating, and unconditional love or infinite hatred, and all other related emotions.
- Majesty—Majesty infers justice and mercy.
- Father of all Virtues—The Father of all virtues is the father of Truth, Honesty, Patience, Temperance, Kindness, Graciousness, Leniency, Humaneness, Gentleness, Tenderness, Benevolence, Charitable, and

Forgiving. The Father of all vices is the father of Lies, Dishonesty, Impatience, Gluttony, Unkindness, Wrath, Pride, Sloth, Lust, Deceit, Greed, and Vindictiveness.

- Happiness—Happiness, gladness, joy, and ecstasy are the result of being compassionate while sorrow, sadness, and depression are the result of cruelty.
- Thankfulness—By being thankful for all we are, all we receive, and all the blessings of our lives, we love and accept ourselves and others more and more. We also become happier, more joyful, and more loving. By being resentful for all we do not have, all that we do not receive, and the curses of our lives, we hate and abhor ourselves and others more and more and we become more anxious, depressed, and filled with rage.

The Function of the Path of Compassion

The Sphere of Compassion is the place within us where we express all variations of all the extremes between absolute hatred and unconditional love. This sphere is where we take all the information from our World of Air and reason it all out on the Path of Reason before we emotionally express our compassion or cruelty as we feel it at this moment and in these circumstances.

The goal of a spiritual warrior is to overcome the "negative" expressions of compassion and express only those considered by society to be "positive." This means most of us have a lot of inner work to do to express the positive aspects of compassion and cruelty in our lives.

We all find it difficult to love a despicable person, like a person who rapes and murders a child or a preadolescent, an adolescent, a young adult, a mature adult, or an elderly person. Such an act offends most of us and it is difficult for us to see any good in such a person. Most of us find it difficult to find any value of any kind in such a person.

But if we knew such acts were committed only by people suffering a terrible mental disease, we might be more merciful and forgiving. If we knew the perpetrator was under the control of another person, demon or entity, we might be more compassionate.

Our ability to reason through all of our thoughts, ideas, memories, imaginings, intentions, and beliefs is what determines our capacity to be compassionate or cruel in any situation at any time. Some prejudiced individuals actually believe that harming other people, the environment, or anything in this world is justified. We may not agree with them or understand their thinking, but we have to live in this world with them.

Our personal spiritual journey demands that we become more compassionate and less cruel. But if we want to survive, this world demands that we accept terrible things a kind and loving person would never consider doing most of the time. We accept war but war is based on the negative emotions of hatred, antipathy, vengeance, and retaliation. We accept death penalties and incarceration based on these same emotions.

In accepting these things, they become a part of us. This is not an indictment against humanity. It's a statement of undeniable truth. But the good news is that the more we inculcate compassion into our lives, the more compassionate and loving we become, the happier and more joyful we become.

By the same token, the more hateful and cruel we become the more depressed, sad, and sorrowful we become. It's entirely up to us. It's a decision we make.

As with all things concerning the Tree of Life we are compassionate on the unconscious, subconscious, and conscious levels of our being. On the conscious level, we are unaware of many things both our subconscious and unconscious minds know. We can learn a little about these higher levels of consciousness by observing how we express compassion in our lives.

The Law of Compassion

The more we express compassion, love, virtue, happiness, mercy, joy, and thankfulness in our lives, the more we become compassionate, loving, happy, merciful, joyful, and thankful and the more we draw these things into our lives.

Lesson 5: The Red Sphere

The red sphere is our personal Sphere of Power. It is the center of our ability to empower ourselves on the unconscious, subconscious, and conscious levels of our being. It is our source of personal power.

The Path of Power

The Sphere of Power is also called by several other names, including:

- The Sphere of Anxiety—Anxiety is the root of our power if we use it to find the inner strength to overcome whatever is causing us anxiety. That's called Freedom. Anxiety is an extreme condition of fear. If we do not overcome our anxiety we become more and more impotent and less and less empowered.
- The Sphere of Empowerment—We empower ourselves by overcoming our fears. We free ourselves by overcoming our fears. Empowering ourselves is freeing ourselves from our fears. This means that if we use our inner strength to overcome whatever we fear, we are finding our power, we are free, we are free from fear.
- The Sphere of Severity—Severity is the power of force. When force is used against us we suffer the pain of severity. Most spiritual paths consider this the root of all evil. But since we live in the World of Duality, we have the ability to find ways to express Gentleness instead of Severity.
- Pachad—Since Pachad is the Hebrew word for fear, this sphere is also the Sphere of Fear or the Sphere of Anxiety. Or we can overcome our fear and anxiety by becoming a Spiritual Warrior.
- The Sphere of the Spiritual Warrior—Spiritual Warriors overcome fear, anxiety, and evil in their lives and the lives of others. They find their power and they "fight for right." The Path of the Spiritual Warrior is the opposite of the Sphere of Pachad.
- Geburah—It Thisis the Hebrew name for the Sphere of Severity or the Sphere of Power.
- The Sphere of Freedom—Freedom from terror, anxiety, fear, worry, and concern is liberating and emancipating. It is liberty and independence. It gives us flexibility and the ability to be free. The Sphere of Freedom is the opposite of the Sphere of Anxiety.

We empower ourselves by becoming free from terror, anxiety, horror, dismay, fear, worry, apprehension, and concern. We empower ourselves by becoming fearless, brave, courageous, daring, unafraid, confident, indomitable, peaceful, and serene.

We become more and more impotent by refusing to empower ourselves and by allowing our terror, anxiety, horror, dismay, fear, worry, apprehension and concerns to multiply, and emotionally paralyze us.

The Function of the Path of Power

The Sphere of Power is the Sphere of Severity and Gentleness. It is the Sphere of Anxiety and Freedom. The attributes of this sphere are as follows:

- Fear, anxiety, worry, concern, apprehension, terror, horror, dismay and nightmarish terror.
- Fearless, brave, courageous, daring, unafraid, confident, indomitable, peaceful, serene, nonviolent, and tranquil.
- And everything in-between.
- Freedom, liberty, independence, emancipation, and flexibility.

Armed with our freedom of choice we have the ability to choose how we will express our own personal power. Everybody does. Every family, community, and government does. How we choose to express our power as an individual, family, group, community, or country is an expression of our intentions and beliefs. It is also an expression of our spiritual path.

We empower ourselves by being fearless, brave, courageous, daring, unafraid, confident, indomitable, peaceful, and serene to the best of our ability at all times and under all circumstances. The more we can attain these virtues in our life, the more we empower ourselves. The more we can attain these virtues, the more we draw people, places, and things into our lives that empower us more and more.

The more we suffer from feelings of nightmarish terror, horror, anxiety, dismay, fear, worry, concerns, or apprehension, the more we become impotent and less empowered. The more impotent we become, the more we draw people, places, and things into our life to make us more and more impotent and less and less empowered. We will continue to draw more and more of these feelings into our lives until we decide to change our attitudes, intentions, and beliefs.

The Law of Power

The Law of Power states that as we overcome our terror, anxiety, worry, concern, and fear we seize our personal power. The more fearless, brave, courageous, peaceful, nonviolent, and tranquil we become the more we draw these things into our lives and empower ourselves. The corollary is that the more we help others overcome these emotions the more we help them empower their selves.

Lesson 6: The Yellow Sphere

The yellow sphere is the Sphere of Harmony. It is the sixth path on the Tree of Life. It is fed by five paths from above and it feeds three paths below. It supports as many paths as the Spheres of Compassion (Path four) and Power (Path five) combined.

The Sphere of Harmony

The Sphere of Harmony has many other names including:

- Tifereth—also spelled Tiphareth or Tiphereth—which is a Hebrew word meaning beauty. Harmony is considered beautiful and it creates beauty all around it. Discord and disharmony do not create beauty all around them. The ancients saw beauty in all things spiritual; and human beings who attain harmony within themselves are beautiful human beings. They also saw discord in all things nonspiritual; and the human beings who followed paths leading away from spirituality.
- *The Sphere of Balance*—or the Sphere of Equilibrium—alludes to the balance within that we call harmony or the lack of balance within which we call discord. It alludes to the fact this sphere is a point of balance between the Sphere of Compassion (blue sphere) and the Sphere of Power (red sphere). It also alludes to the fact this sphere is the balance point between the Worlds Above and the Worlds Below.
- *Melek* is a Hebrew word meaning King. The ancients attributed this word to this sphere because the Kingdom at the bottom of the Tree of Life is under the influence of the power or powerlessness of this sphere. This sphere is also called the King of Manifestation. The Sphere of Melek is the Sphere of the King. The King is a symbol of the range of authority from beneficial to malefic.
- *The Sphere of Adam or the Sphere of The Son.* This alludes to the ancient concept that the Sphere of Harmony is the male child of the marriage between Father Intentions (gray sphere) and Mother Beliefs (black sphere) consummated by Creator Awareness (the white sphere).

In ancient times this was called the immaculate conception or the unclean conception.

- *The Child* is another name for the Sphere of Adam but it alludes to the fact that everything in the creation is a child of the Divine. The child is also called the Christ Child, the Buddha Child, the Child Krishna, and several other names alluding to religious leaders. Thus this center is also called the Sphere of Christ, Sphere of Buddha, and the Sphere of Lord Krishna.

- *The Door to Heaven and Hell* is a way of explaining that our own higher self resides above the Sphere of Harmony while our lower self resides in the paths and spheres below. Everything above this sphere is called the Above and everything below is called the Below. Some people believe Above is Heaven and Below is Hell. The Sphere of Harmony is also called the Gates to Heaven and Hell.

- *Sphere of the Mystic* is also called the Sphere of the Adept. Both titles allude to the fact that the Sphere of Harmony is mystical. As we move up the Tree of Life from the bottom, we start out in the multicolored sphere as a conscious being. When we move up the Tree to the next sphere we do so by developing our psychic abilities. We move up into the Sphere of Harmony by developing our mystical abilities. This is our ability to commune directly with the Divine, to tune into the Divine essence, to become a mystic and an adept.

- *The Sphere of Healing and Illness* explains why and how people are able to heal themselves of all kinds of physical, mental, emotional and psychological conditions, diseases, and disorders by raising their vibration up to the Gates of Heaven. A common attribute of all saints, adepts, and mystics is their ability to help people heal themselves in this manner. But this is also the Sphere of Illness for those of us who do not heal. This is because all healing of all kinds is a personal choice.

- *Sphere of the Sun* attribution is based on the fact that all healing gods of all religions are Sun Gods and all Sun Gods are healing gods. To the best of my knowledge, there is no Sun God that is not a healing god and there are no healing gods that are not Sun Gods. It's also interesting to observe the fact this sphere is attributed to the Sun by the Cabala.

This is not the time nor place to discuss the immaculate conception. Suffice it to say that between the time of the earliest writings on this topic and the birth of the child Jesus there are several so-called "myths" that speak of the immaculate conception of several "gods." There are at least three ways of looking at this information: (1) immaculate conception is a myth and not a fact, (2) immaculate conception is a fact in one case and a myth in all others, or (3) immaculate conception is not a unique experience.

The Path of Harmony is the Path of Peace. The more harmonious we are with ourselves and everything else in the creation the more peaceful, peace-loving, serene, peaceable, calm, non-violent, pleased, tranquil, accommodating, and appeased we feel. The more peaceful we feel, the more we draw people, places, and things into our life to increase our inner peace and calm. The more inner peace and calm we attain, the more spiritual we become.

The Path of Discord is the Path of Wrath. The more discordant we feel about ourselves and everything in the creation, the more we are filled with wrath, rage, fury, anger, irritation, agitation, and annoyance. The more we feel these emotions, the more we draw people, places, and things into our life to support these feelings and increase our anger, fury, rage, and wrath. The more inner anger and rage we attain the further we move away from a spiritual path, the further we move away from the peace and joy of the Divine.

The Function of the Sphere of Harmony

The Sphere of Harmony is where we balance everything in our life according to our Intentions and Beliefs. It is the sphere of our wrath, rage, anger, irritation, and agitation. It is also our sphere of calmness, peace, harmony, content, and serenity.

The Law of Harmony

The Law of Harmony states we have the right and the ability to be balanced, content, at peace and calm; and we have the ability to be free, independent, happy, and compassionate.

Lesson 7: The Green Sphere

The Green Sphere is the Sphere of Desire. It is Path seven on the Tree of Life. The Hebrew name of this sphere is Netzach which means Firmness but is usually translated as Victory. The opposites of these are Softness and Defeat. Path seven is the Element of Fire in the World of Fire.

The Path of Desire

The Path of Desire has a few other recognized names including:

- The Path of Victory—We are victorious when we subdue our passions, but we are defeated when our passions conquer us.
- The Path of Fire—This is the path of plans, wants, needs, desires, passions, cravings, addictions, obsessions, and energy.
- The Path of Selflessness—The Path of Desire is considered to be selfless and unselfish, but it can also be selfish and driven by an overpowering ego.

The Function of the Path of Desire

The Element of Fire is the element of energy expressed as plans, wants, needs, desires, passions, cravings, obsessions, and addictions. At its best, the Element of Fire is the Path of Plans, Wants, Needs, Desires, and Passions. At its worse, the Element of Fire is cravings, obsessions, and addictions. Thus Path seven can also be called the Path of Passions and Cravings.

Because Path seven is also located in the World of Fire, this gives a lot of energy to our plans, wants, needs, desires, passions, cravings, obsessions, and addictions. When we intelligently and compassionately manage this energy of Fire, we are able to manifest our plans, satisfy our wants, needs, desires and passions, and we are able to avoid cravings addictions and obsessions.

When we are not able to manage this energy of Fire, that same Fire energy converts our passions and desires into cravings, addictions, and obsessions. We are not in control. We are at the mercy of our uncontrolled Fire energy.

The Law of Desire

The Law of Desire says we can acquire, attain, and become what we truly desire only when our desires are in complete accord with our Worlds of Air, Reflection, Water, and Within.

- We are in accord with our World of Air when we Intend to do what we believe we can do. We are in accord with our World of Water when our Compassion, Harmony and Inner Power are in complete agreement with our desire. We are in accord with all our Worlds when our Spirit and Soul are in agreement with our desire.

Lesson 8: The Orange Sphere

The orange sphere is the Sphere of Competency. It is the eighth path on the Tree of Life. The Hebrew name for this sphere is Hod which means Glory. According to the ancients, the Glory of the Divine is its glorious Mind. Our glory is our glorious intellect.

The Path of Competency

The Path of Competency has a few other recognized names including:

- Path of Glory—According to the Kaballah the Path of Glory is the Path of Form. The suggestion here is that we create our own form with our mind and this is the Glory of Manifestation, the Glory of the Divine Plan.
- The Path of Air—This is the path of information in the form of thoughts and ideas, intentions and beliefs, awareness, focus of attention, memory and imagination, attitudes, words, and pictures.
- The Path of Intellect—A good Intellect is an asset and a poor Intellect can be a burden to one's family and self.
- The Path of Genius and Ignorance—This is another name for the path of Intellect or Intelligence.

The Function of the Path of Competency

The Path of Competency is the Path of Air in the World of Fire. It is the intellectual center for Astral World. As such it represents thoughts and ideas with energy behind them. This energy comes from the World of Fire. Without this energy we could never manifest our intentions and beliefs. With this energy we have the possibility of manifesting our intentions and beliefs.

The Path of Competency is the Path of Intellect and the Path of Intelligence. This path is the center of consciousness for our ego. This is the center of our mental functioning, learning, and communication. This is the mind we have manifested in this world and that mind can be genius or challenged.

The Path of Glory is explained as the reflection of the Path of Compassion which itself is a reflection of the Path of our beliefs. What this means is that our form is determined by our beliefs as they are reflected by our Compassion and our mental capacity for creating our own body.

The Law of Competency

The Law of Competency teaches us that we have the ability to do and learn what we came into this existence to do and learn regardless of appearances to the contrary.

Lesson 9: The Violet Sphere

The Violet Sphere is the Sphere of Enthusiasm. In Hebrew it is called Yesod which means "foundation." Yesod is the Foundation of the World and the foundation of the world is the Astral World. The Astral "stuff" is the foundation or framework upon which the material universe is built. But Foundation has another meaning and that is the emotional stability that allows material universe to function. Our own emotional stability is the foundation of our own personality.

The Path of Enthusiasm

The Path of Enthusiasm has a few other recognized names including:

- Foundation—This refers to the foundation on which the physical reality is built. That foundation is the Path of Enthusiasm.
- The Foundation of the World—This is another name for Foundation.
- The Astral World—The Foundation of the World is the Astral World which is the Foundation of the manifested world.
- The World of Emotions—The Path of Enthusiasm is the Emotional Element in the World of Fire.
- The Path of Water—Water is the Emotional Element represented by the Path of Enthusiasm in the World of Fire.

The Function of the Path of Enthusiasm

The Path of Enthusiasm is the expression of emotions in the World of Fire. The World of Fire is the world of our plans, wants, needs, desires, passions, cravings, obsessions, and addictions. The Element of Water expresses our emotions in this World of Fire. The emotions we can express in the World of Fire are all of the emotions we develop in our own World of Water:

- Compassion includes happiness, gladness, joy, ecstasy, sorrow, sadness, caring and not-caring, nurturing and retaliating, unconditional love and infinite hatred, thankfulness and resentment, revenge, vindictiveness, and unconditionally loving.
- Power includes terror, anxiety, horror, dismay, fear, worry, apprehension, concern, fearless, brave, courageous, daring, unafraid, confident, indomitable, peaceful, and serene.
- Harmony includes peaceful, peace-loving, serene, peaceable, calm, nonviolent, pleased, tranquil, accommodating, appeased, wrath, rage, fury, anger, irritation, agitation, and annoyance.
- Enthusiasm is contagious because it generates excitement, warmth, and passion. It can result in frenzy, fervor, zeal, vehemence, inspiration, and devotion. It generates energy.
- Indifference is a cold rag that shuts down enthusiasm and leads to callousness, repugnance, alienation, and contempt. It is the opposite of caring, nurturing, and affection. It uses up energy.
- Any combination or variation of the above.

The Law of Enthusiasm

The Law of Enthusiasm says that where you place your energy is what you manifest and bring into your life.

Lesson 10: The Multicolored Sphere

The multicolored sphere at the bottom of the Tree of Life is the Sphere of Manifestation. It is Path ten on the Tree of Life. The Hebrew name of this sphere is Malkuth which means the Kingdom. This tenth sphere on the Tree of Life is the Kingdom of the Divine.

The Path of Manifestation

The Path of Manifestation is known by several other names including the Gate, the Gate of Death, the Gate of the Shadow of Death, the Gate of Tears, the Gate of Justice, the Gate of Prayer, the Gate of the Garden of Eden, and the Gate of Heaven and Hell. It is also called the Virgin, Bride, Queen, and Inferior Mother. This last title alludes to the Sphere of Beliefs which is called the Supernal Mother.

The four colors attributed to Manifestation represent the four Elements of Earth at the bottom, Air at the top, Fire on the observer's left, and Water on the right. This intended to convey the idea that the other three Elements residing in the World of Fire, the Astral World, are reflected into the World of Earth where they manifest as our Intellect (Air), Emotions (Water), and Drive (Fire).

We express ourselves in the Manifestation on the conscious level of our being. Our subconscious mind is partially hidden from us. Our unconscious mind is almost completely hidden from us. This handicaps us and forces us to learn more about ourselves and everything in the creation with limited resources.

The ancient wisdom of the Tree of Life teaches us that this is necessary for our spiritual advancement. Otherwise we would continue to exist in complete knowing. When you already know everything you cannot learn anything.

The Function of the Path of Manifestation

This Path is the fulfillment of the whole creative process. It is the manifestation in the World of Earth of our Awareness, Intentions, Beliefs, Compassion, Power, Harmony, Desire, Competency, and Enthusiasm. If that manifestation isn't what we want it to be, then we need to look at how we are handling these other aspects of our consciousness and being, because that's where the problem is.

The Law of Manifestation

The Law of Manifestation says that the world we experience is the manifestation of our state of consciousness, as it descends through the first nine spheres of the Tree of Life.

CHAPTER 5

Tarot and Spirituality

1. The Tree of Life and the Wheel of the Year

In every religion, known to me, there's a creation story that explains how this world and all within it came into being. The story is different from culture to culture and from time to time, but one theme seems to be very consistent in all creation stories. This theme suggests that in the beginning there was nothing except the Creator who created everything which was ever created.

How the Creator created this world and everything in it is explained differently by different religions. But again, there is a common theme running through the story. Both Eastern and Western religions look on creation as a vertical process from above to below. The Northern and Southern religions look on creation as a circle that goes around and around. The Judeo–Christian–Islamic religions refer to this process as the Tree of Life, and the Pagan–Earth–Spirit religions refer to it as the Circle of Life or Wheel of the Year. Despite the bickering between religious groups, it seems to me the Tree and Circle are both the same thing.

The Tree of Life can be depicted in many different ways. So can the Circle of Life or the Wheel of the Year. My approach will be to look at both of them side by side in several different ways so we can start to gain some insight into the Creative Mind. As we gain this insight into Deity, we learn more about ourselves and our own spiritual journey.

Both the Tree and the Circle start with the premise of an all-powerful Source which created everything that exists in all worlds and places. Various religions describe this Source as having no form, being formless, existing without shape or mass, having no size or consisting of nothing, no matter, no energy, just intelligence. Intelligence existing without form constitutes a point and a point is the beginning of both the Tree of Life and the Circle of Life.

The Circle of Life starts with a point in space. From this point energy expands outward in eight spokes of the wheel. The first spoke expands above constituting a line with going outward from the central point. This first line is considered masculine in nature and is equivalent to the Lord of Life or the Lord of the Circle of Life. The second spoke expands at a ninety-degree angle to the first and is considered feminine in nature and is equivalent to the Lady of Life or the Lady of the Circle of Life. The third spoke is in the opposite direction of the second and is also feminine in nature and is equivalent to the Daughter of the Circle of Life or the Lady in Waiting. This is the immature feminine energy which one day will be the Lady of the Circle of Life. The fourth spoke is in the opposite direction of the first and is considered masculine in nature and is equivalent to the Son of the Circle of Life or the Heir Apparent to the Lord of the Circle. This is immature masculine energy which one day will become the Lord of the Circle of Life.

The Circle of Life is now half completed and consists of five things:

- The central point representing the Creator
- The line above representing the Lord of Life
- The perpendicular line representing the Lady of Life
- The continuation of that perpendicular line representing the Daughter
- The continuation of the vertical line representing the Son

The first half of the Circle of Life looks like a simple cross and represents masculine energy intersecting with feminine. Pagans understand this symbol very well as a representation of the energy of the Lord and Lady of the Universe with the creative energy of the Universe at their intersection.

These same four arms of the cross can also be used to represent the four seasons of the year and the four directions. Above becomes Winter and North. Below becomes Summer and South. To the right becomes Spring and East and to the left becomes Autumn and West. The Summer and Winter Solstices and the Spring and Autumn Equinoxes can also be represented by this same cross. The four elements are also represented by this cross. Earth to the North, Air to the East, Water to the West, and Fire to the South is one possibility. Another is Air to the North, Fire to the South with Water to the West and Earth to the East. This second system is devised to keep the horizontal elements feminine and the vertical elements masculine.

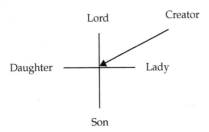

The second part of the circle consists of four more spokes going outward from the center point forming an "X" on the original cross. Some say these four spokes represent four younger children of the Lord and Lady. Their personalities are defined by the two elements on either side of them. If the Lord is Earth and the Lady is Air, the line drawn halfway between them represents an intellectual down-to-earth child. Likewise, the line drawn halfway between the Lord and the Daughter represents an emotional down-to-earth child. The line drawn between the Lady and the Son is a fiery intellectual. And the line drawn between the Son and the Daughter is a fiery emotional child.

Around the Lord and Lady and all their children is a circle which represents a containing barrier which holds everything together. Both the masculine and feminine energies are contained within this outer circle. The outer circle represents the final result of creation, this world, this country, this community, this life, this body, this thing. Each of us is a Circle of Life. Each of us is a Wheel of Time, a Wheel of the Year and of all Years. We form groups that are Circles of Life contained within a larger Circle of Life.

The Circle of Life is now completed and the final five parts are as follows:

- Child of Earth and Air
- Child of Earth and Water
- Child of Fire and Air
- Child of Fire and Water
- Manifestation, the Completion

Our completed Circle of Life is shown in the diagram below.

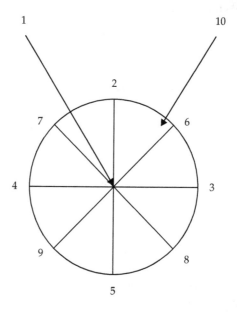

The Tree of Life starts with a point in space. Energy expands outward and downward in two streams of energy from this primal point to form two more points. Each of these points shares energy with the other two forming a triangle in space.

The energy going down what appears to us to be the right-hand path is masculine in nature and the energy going down the other path is its opposite or feminine energy. And by convention, these points in space are considered to be spheres because each of them contains energy. The first point, or sphere, contains the creative energy of the Universe and is often referred to as the Creator God. The second sphere to our right is masculine in nature and can be referred to as

Father God while the third sphere is feminine in nature and can be referred to as Mother God.

Creator God

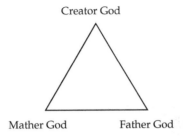

Mather God   Father God

Notice the similarity between this and the Creator, Lord, and Lady of the Circle of life. To me they are one and the same. The Lord is the Father God and the Lady is the Mother God. The names can be used interchangeably. They are the essence of masculine and feminine energies just as the Creator is the essence of creative energy. The Creator came first and the masculine and feminine energies came next and they came from and are a part of the Creator. From these three come all things according to most creation stories in almost all religions. This is the original "Trinity," the three Gods-in-One, the Creator God, the Father God, and the Mother God.

The Father God is often called Wisdom. Because masculine energy goes ever outward it has the opportunity to learn much and become wise. The Mother God is often called Understanding. Because feminine energy contains itself it has the opportunity to learn more and more about a thing and understands it better.

Wisdom gives birth to Charity as the wiser we become the more we realize all of creation is founded on love and only in love can creation continue to grow. Charity is also known as Mercy because love makes us merciful to all others. Understanding gives birth to Anger and Fear or Trepidation because the more we understand life the more we fear the unknown and the angrier we become with that which we fear. These are fundamental emotions between which all people waver from time to time. We shift between understanding and wisdom, between love and anger, between charity and fear, and between mercy and hardness of heart. We seek a middle between them where we can become balanced in all things.

The energy from the spheres of Mercy, Charity or Love on our right and Trepidation, Fear or Anger on our left expand downward toward the center and meet forming a triangle which is a reflection of the first triangle on the Tree of Life. The sphere formed at the junction of these two lines is considered to be a thing of Beauty because here come together our fears and our anger with our charity and our love and we become balanced. To be balanced in all things is a thing of Beauty. This sphere of Beauty is the first sphere where the masculine and feminine energies of the Lord and Lady, Wisdom and Understanding, come together. Beauty is the firstborn Son of the Father and Mother Gods. Some consider the firstborn to be the anointed one, the Christ, the Son of God (Father God and Mother God).

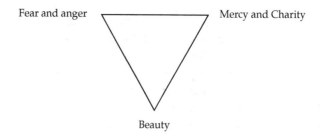

Fear and anger   Mercy and Charity

Beauty

An interesting exercise is to compare these three spheres of Love and Charity, Anger and Fear, and Son and Beauty to the Circle of Life to determine where they fall on the Circle. Placing the Son and Beauty below is fairly easy. Placing the other two is more of a challenge but constitutes an exercise yielding both wisdom and understanding.

Love or Mercy gives birth to Victory or Mastery because as we learn the art of loving ourselves and all things, of extending mercy to ourselves and all others, we gain Victory or Mastery over life. We become the masters of our own destiny. We become masters living in this world but apart from it. Fear and Anger give birth to Glory or Splendor because as we come to understand ourselves, our fears and the source of our anger, we begin to see the Glory that is us and all of creation. We see the Splendor of all that is.

As Charity (Mercy or Love) and Trepidation (Anger or Fear) send out energy which comes together as the Son, so Mastery (or Victory) and Glory (or Splendor) send out their energy to form the Foundation of the World, the Daughter of the Gods. This energy is sent downward from Victory and Splendor toward the center and forms another triangle in a manner similar to the energy sent downward from Mercy and Fear.

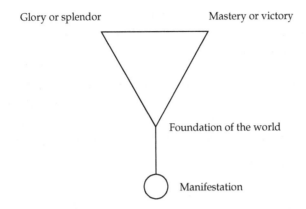

Hanging from Foundation in this third triangle and supported by both Splendor and Victory is Manifestation, the completion of the creation. All the energy from the whole tree flows down into Manifestation not unlike all of the energy of the Circle of Life flowing into the outer rim of the circle.

The similarities between the Tree of Life and the Wheel of the Year are remarkable and time spent seeking out the wisdom and understanding hidden there is usually well spent. A good starting point is to place the labels from the Tree of Life on the Circle of Life and then bring in the festivals of the year to complete the picture.

2. The Three Pillars and the Dagger and Cup

The Wheel of the Year is a circle formed around a point in the center representing the Creator of all that is. From this center a vertical line springs forth above and below. Above represents the Father God and below represents the Son God. This Father–Son line is eternal and expands forever. This expansion is represented by a dagger.

From the center of the Wheel of the Year a horizontal line springs forth to the left and the right. To our right as we look at the Wheel of the Year is the line representing the Mother God and to our left is the Daughter God. While this line looks like a straight line to us, it's really curved to form a bowl. This is because the whole weight of creation rests in the middle of this line. Thus the expansion of the feminine line is represented by a cup, bowl, or a cauldron.

As an aside, modern astronomers are defining the plane of solar systems and galaxies as "curved straight lines" to explain the effect of gravity (the weight of creation) on the stars, planets, and other astronomical bodies (the fruits of creation). It never fails to amaze me how modern science continues to prove ancient knowledge previously considered to be the "Ignorant thoughts of Savage Pagans."

Everything that ever was or ever will be is created at the center of this "Goddess" line where the masculine energies meet the feminine. Creation occurs at this point where the masculine and feminine energies meet. This point represents the Creator of all that is.

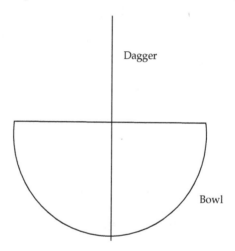

This symbol of the Cup and the Dagger represents the creative influence in the Universe. It also represents the creative energies of the male and female in human society. When used in this manner, some say the Son is being conceived and is not yet born. The result of the commingling of the masculine and feminine will be the Son. Others claim the masculine energy is the Son becoming the Father.

By the same token, the Cup can be considered to be the Daughter becoming the Mother. The Cup can also represent the conception of the Daughter. In some religions it is the conception of both the Son and the Daughter. The God and the Goddess meet at the point of creation and all life springs forth both male and female.

The Cup can be considered to have a left side and a right side as we look at it. The Mother God (Air) is at the right-hand edge of the straight line defining the top of the cup. The Daughter God (Water) is at the left-hand edge. The Son God (Fire) is at the bottom of the Cup and the Father God (Earth) is above the Cup.

If we consider the right-hand side of the Cup as we stand back and look at the Cup, we see the Mother God on the right and the Son God at the bottom with the Creator at the top.

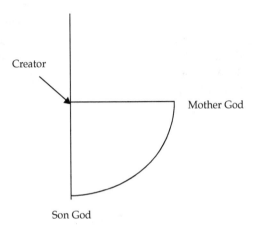

Creator

Mother God

Son God

This portion of the Cup defines the Creator God as the focal point above the Son God and on the same level as the Mother God. The three elements here are Spirit, Air, and Fire. Spirit supports both Fire and Air. Air supports Fire and Fire is friendly to Air. This is the same thing as saying the Creator God supports both Mother and Son and the Mother and Son are friendly toward one another. All in all, this is a very harmonious and positive relationship.

This right-handed cup could be called the Cup of Mercy, Cup of Love (or the Love Cup), or the Cup of Charity, Peace, Encouragement, Growth, or Abundance. It is a cup of optimistic, nurturing, positive energy. It nourishes the soul, brings us peace, love, and tranquility. It could be, and is, called by many positive names in many cultures.

Likewise, the left-hand side of the Cup represents the Daughter God on the left, the Son God below and the Creator God at the top opposite the Daughter God and above the Son God.

This portion of the Cup defines the Creator God as the focal point above the Son and on the same level as the Daughter. The Three elements are Spirit, Fire, and Water. Spirit supports both Fire and Water. Water and Fire are hostile toward each other and not at all friendly. All in all, this is an inimical and very negative relationship.

This left-handed cup could be called the Cup of Disaster, Cup of Bile, or the Cup of Conflict, Animosity, Fear, Anger, Death, Weakness, and

Wanting. It is a cup of pessimistic, repulsive, negative energy. It destroys our self-image, brings us turmoil, pain, and suffering. It could be, and is, called by many derogatory names.

It seems to me these two portions of the Cup are very similar to the Right and Left Pillars on the Tree of Life. The Right-hand Pillar on the Tree of Life is defined by the Father God above, Mercy or Charity in the Middle, and Victory or Mastery below. The Left-hand Pillar is defined by the Mother God above, Fear and Anger in the Middle, and Glory or Splendor below.

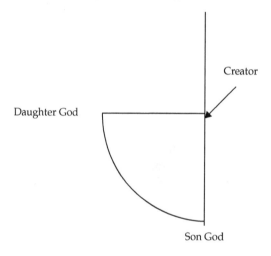

The Right Pillar is often called the Pillar of Wisdom or the Pillar of Mercy. But it has many other names including Pillar of Fire, Charity, Victory, Health or Healing, Forgiveness, Benevolence, and other positive, nurturing optimistic, and loving names.

The Left Pillar is often called the Pillar of Strength. But it has many other names including the Cloud Pillar, the Pillar of Severity, Fear, Anger, Malevolence, Cruelty, Unkindness, Intolerance, Arrogance, Wrath, and other negative, pessimistic, and hateful names.

The Right Pillar and the Right-handed Cup seem, to me, to represent the same qualities of life. The Left Pillar and the Left-handed Cup also seem to represent the same things. Is it possible many different cultures around the world devised many different ways of interpreting the same things? Is it possible the Celtic Pagans of Europe and the Asiatic peoples independently developed the Wheel of the Year and the Cup and Dagger while the Middle Easterners were developing their concepts of the Tree of Life? Is it possible the Tree of Life and the Cup and Dagger explain mankind's understanding of the World of Opposites? The World of Good and Evil in which we find ourselves living?

To me it's more than just possible, that's exactly what happened. In our attempts to explain the unexplainable we created images of cups and daggers, trees and pillars and we explained things that cannot be explained. We explained the uncertainties of life on the one hand and our dreams and accomplishments on the other. We drew a picture of good and evil. We incorporated these things into our language, rituals, and culture.

The Right-handed and Left-handed Cups come together to form the Cup of Creation, the Manifested Cup, the Cup of Life. This Cup is the world in which we live, a world of good and bad, love and anger, charity and hatred. This is the World of the Right and Left Pillars of the Tree of Life. This is the World of Opposites, man and woman, male and female.

But our ancient brethren knew there was more to life than this. They postulated a world of balance in the middle between love and hatred, good and bad, male and female, positive and negative. This middle is the point of creation where the dagger meets the cup. This is a point where all things come together and perfect balance exists. It is represented by the Dagger.

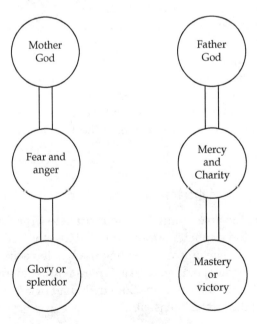

A different group of our ancient brethren contemplating the same problem arrived at the same conclusion and defined this point of balance in the middle as the Middle Pillar of the Tree of Life. To me, both groups saw and understood the same things but arrived at different symbols to explain them. One group called this point of absolute balance the Dagger of Manifestation, Dagger of Life and Death, Dagger of Creation, and the Sword of God. The other group called it the Pillar of Beauty, Pillar of Life and Death, Pillar of Creation, and the Throne of God. Both have several different names in different cultures and religions.

An interesting exercise is to compare the ten spheres of the Tree of Life as they are placed on the Three Pillars with the ten parts of the Wheel of the Year as they are placed on the Cup and the Dagger. Then assign the ten ranks of the pip cards in the Minor Arcana to these same ten spheres or parts. Finally, assign the sixteen court cards to four of the spheres or parts. One way to get started is to assign the Aces to the first point of creation, the beginning, and proceed to the Tens which are assigned to the last phase of creation represented by the final sphere or the all-encompassing circle that contains everything else. The Kings and Queens can be placed on the Father and Mother Gods aspects, respectively. The Pages and Knights can be placed on the Daughter and Son aspects, respectively.

The Major Arcana can also be placed on the Cup and Dagger or the Tree of Life. This can be done in many ways and no one way appears to be superior to any other method of placement. Each system of placement has strengths and weaknesses. Each can be justified in various ways. Much can be learned about one's self and the creative principles behind everything by experimenting with various placements of the Major Arcana on both the Tree of Life and the Wheel of the Year.

3. The Triads of the Tree and the Quadrants of the Wheel

The spheres of the Tree of Life form four triangles. The first triangle is formed by the three spheres attributed to the Creator God, Father God, and Mother God. This upward-pointing triangle looks like the symbol we use for the element of Fire. Kabalists normally assign the element of Fire to this triangle and call it the Supernal Triad or the First Creation. It's also called the First Dimension.

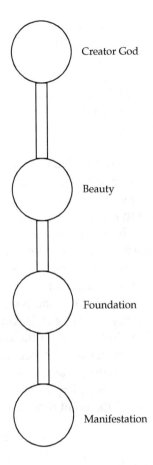

Creator God

Beauty

Foundation

Manifestation

The First Dimension is the Causal World which causes all things to come into being by an act of will, intention, and determination. Will, intention, and determination define the element of Fire. It represents potential energy and potential form or matter.

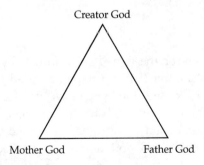

Creator God

Mother God   Father God

In the Wheel of the Year, also called the Circle of Life (See Fig. 2), the element of Fire is assigned to the southern quadrant and the direction South. This is where the Sun resides during the hot days of Summer. This section of the Wheel of the Year is defined by lines drawn between 1–8–5–9–1 on the Circle of Life. This upward-pointing, pie-shaped wedge is the domain of the Son. While he rules the year, all things grow and multiply. Children, crops, and livestock grow and thrive during this time.

This quadrant is defined by the Creator, the Son, the Child of Fire and Air, and the Child of Fire and Water. This is not the Causal World of pure Fire, it's an Emotional World of Air, Fire, and Water. Air fans the Fire while Water tries to quench the flames. The Son has his hands full with his two children. In mythology, these are the children of the Son and the Lady and the Son and his parent's Daughter. The Son has committed double incest. For this sin he must ultimately be slain. Few things could be more emotional than that.

On the surface, the First Triad and the South Quadrant look like two different worlds. However, both are upward pointing and both represent the element Fire. Both represent the act of creation albeit in different ways. Both balance the conflict between opposites. On the Tree of Life, Mother God balances Father God. The Creator God is the point of balance between them. On the Circle of Life, the Children balance each other. The Son is the point of balance between them.

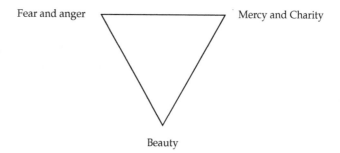

Fear and anger

Mercy and Charity

Beauty

The second triangle on the Tree of Life is formed by the three spheres representing the "children" of the Supernal Triad. This downward-pointing triangle looks like the symbol we use for Water. Kabalists normally assign the element of Water to this triangle and call it the Ethical Triangle, the Second Trinity, and the Second Creation. It's also called the Emotional World and represents the Second Dimension.

In the beginning is the will to create, but before anything can become manifest, love, or emotion, must be added to the equation. This is the Second Creation—adding emotion to the determination to create.

Emotion is the element of Water. Fear and Anger are emotions. Mercy and Charity are a decision based on the emotion of Love just as Unmerciful and Uncharitable acts are committed under the influence of the emotions of Fear and Anger. Thus Mercy and Charity balance Fear and Anger just as Mother God balances Father God. The point of balance is Beauty which also represents the Son God.

On the Circle of Life, the West Quadrant representing Water is defined by the lines drawn between 1–9–4–7–1 on the Circle of Life. This quadrant is defined by the Creator, the Daughter, the Child of Water and Earth, and the Child of Water and Fire. Notice the Child of Fire and Water and the Creator are both common to this quadrant and the preceding one. But this time the Fire is not fanned by Air, rather it is quenched by both Water and Earth.

On the Circle of Life, the East Quadrant is the World of Air defined by the lines drawn between 1–6–3–8–1 on the Circle of Life. This quadrant is defined by the Creator, Mother, Child of Earth and Air, and the Child of Fire and Air. Notice the conflict which arises as the Air fans the flames of Fire while Earth quenches the Fire. Earth and Fire balance each other and Air rules this quadrant just as Earth and Fire balance each other in the Water Quadrant.

There are good arguments for assigning either quadrant to the Second Triad on the Tree of Life. The Air Quadrant and Emotional Triangle both represent Spring. The Water Quadrant and the Emotional Triangle both represent Water. It's also interesting to look at the symbols. The Fourth Quadrant defined by lines drawn between 1–7–2–6–1 forms a downward-pointing, pie-shaped wedge similar to the downward-pointing triangle used as a symbol for Water.

Thus any of these three quadrants could be attributed to the Ethical Triangle on the Tree of Life. This points out an interesting phenomenon common to all systems of attributing one paradigm to another: there are many different ways of making those attributions. It seems to me we grow in both wisdom and understanding as we change these attributions from time to time and justify our new choices. For now, let's assign the Water Quadrant, the home of the Daughter, to the Second Triangle which represents the Mother of Creation and Water.

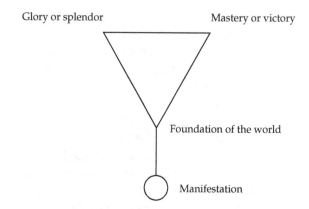

Glory or splendor   Mastery or victory

Foundation of the world

Manifestation

The third triangle on the Tree of Life is formed by the three spheres Glory, Mastery and the Foundation. This triangle is called the Third Triad, the Third Creation, the Astral World and the Personality Triangle. It represents the Third Dimension and the World of Air. The original will to create which has become an emotional desire to create now plans and visualizes this creation in the World of the Mind. On a personal level, first comes the determination to procreate, then when emotion is added to the mixture, this determination becomes a desire to procreate. Reason is added to the equation and finally, the act of procreation comes to pass.

Glory, Splendor, Mastery, and Victory are all created in the mind. Without ideas and thought there is no glory, no victory, no splendor, and no mastery. Yet, Victory and Glory balance each other as do Mastery and Splendor. Victory results in Glory. Mastery results in Splendor. The Foundation of the World is the balance point between these opposites. This downward-pointing triangle mimics the preceding triangle.

If we continue to use the symbol as our basis for mapping the Triads on the Tree of Life to the Quadrants on the Wheel of the Year, we could choose to map the Third Triad to the Fourth Quadrant. Both are downward-pointing symbols. Both can be assigned to the World of Air.

That brings up another interesting thing about attributing one group of symbols to another. We said earlier the element of Fire was assigned to the Quadrant of the Son. Fire can also be assigned to the Quadrant of the Lord. Either masculine element can be attributed to either masculine figure. Likewise, Water could be matched with either the Lady or the Daughter. Add to this mix the four directions of East,

West, North, and South and assign them to the elements and then to the masculine and feminine figures. The number of possible combinations staggers the mind.

Yet, wisdom and understanding can be reached only by delving into the mysteries of these things. The more a person works with these concepts the more he or she learns about himself or herself and the whole Universe. Out of frustration is born understanding and out of the love for it all comes wisdom. Here's another attribution:

> First Triad = North = Fire = Lord
> Second Triad = West = Water = Daughter
> Third Triad = South = Air = Son
> Fourth Triad = East = Earth = Lady

Here's a third possibility:

> First Triad = East = Air = Lady
> Second Triad = South = Fire = Son
> Third Triad = West = Water = Daughter
> Fourth Triad = North = Earth = Lord

And, yet a fourth:

> First Triad = Father = Fire = East
> Second Triad = Mother = Water = West
> Third Triad = Son = Air = South
> Fourth Triad = Daughter = Earth = North

For our purposes, let's continue assigning the Triads to the Quadrants on the basis of the Elements and using the attributions we've been discussing. In this case, Air is the element for the Third Triad and the Quadrant of the Lady. This quadrant is defined by lines drawn between 1–6–3–8–1.

The fourth triangle is drawn using the spheres Glory, Victory, and Manifestation. Some Kabalists use only the final sphere and divide it into four parts. An element is assigned to each of these four parts. The first three parts receive Air, Fire, and Water from above in the Tree and the combination of these forms the fourth part which is Earth. Either way, the final sphere or Fourth Triad is assigned to the element of Earth. This is the physical reality in which we all live. This is the Fourth Creation, the World of Matter, the Fourth Dimension. This world we assign to the Lord, the Lord of Earth, the King of the Kingdom.

According to ancient wisdom, time exists only in the manifested world. In the higher worlds there is only an eternal now. The Wheel of Life goes round and round in this physical world. The Lord is dead. Long live the Lord. There's always another lord to take the place of the one who just died. So it is with all things. But in the eternal present we all exist for all time.

That's the promise of all spiritual paths, that all of us are eternal. We existed before the Tree of Life and the Wheel of the Year. We are the Tree of Life and the Wheel of the Year. But when those things pass away and are no more, we remain. We are forever.

INDEX

CPSIA information can be obtained
at www.ICGtesting.com
Printed in the USA
JSHW010932210223
38007JS00005B/8